Updated with additional notes and a new expanded scoresheet

FAMILY CHILD CARE ENVIRONMENT RATING SCALE

REVISED EDITION

THELMA HARMS   **DEBBY CRYER**   **RICHARD M. CLIFFORD**

Frank Porter Graham Child Development Institute
The University of North Carolina at Chapel Hill

TEACHERS COLLEGE PRESS

Teachers College, Columbia University
New York and London

Published by Teachers College Press, 1234 Amsterdam Avenue, New York, NY 10027

Cover design by Warren McCollum

ISBN 978-0-8077-4725-4

Printed on acid-free paper

Manufactured in the United States of America

14   13   12   11   10   09   08   07   8   7   6   5   4   3   2   1

Contents

124150

Acknowledgments

Over the years, our work has been enriched by the many colleagues in the United States, Canada, Europe, and Asia who have used the *Family Day Care Rating Scale* in research, program improvement, and monitoring, and have generously shared their insights with us. We want especially to thank the many people who responded to our questionnaire with ideas for this revision. We received hundreds of responses and read and considered every suggestion, and although it is not possible to thank each one of you personally, we want you to know how meaningful your guidance was as we considered revisions.

We want to recognize in particular:

- Lisa Waller and Elisa Allen who so ably coordinated and directed the field test.
- The observers who collected the field test data and, at the end of the field test, gave us their valuable critique: Elisa Allen, Lisa Waller, Keisha Neal, Cathy Riley, Tracy Link, Kristina Lee, Stephanie Shreve, and Syndee Kraus.
- Special thanks to Lisa Waller, Elisa Allen, Keisha Neal, Cathy Riley, Tracy Link, and Syndee Kraus for detailed feedback and valuable suggestions.
- Elisa Allen for her attention to detail in preparing the manuscript, and Lisa Waller for her work in revising the Expanded Scoresheet.

- Marie Ellen Larcada, our editor at Teachers College Press, for her patience and determination.
- Susan Liddicoat for copyediting our manuscript so ably.
- Stephanie Shreve and Diane Early for their careful analysis of the field test data.
- Vanessa Loiselle and Ashley Harden for providing administrative support.
- Family child care providers and technical assistance personnel and many others working with family child care for responding to our survey about needed revisions.
- Family child care providers across North Carolina, for playing a very important role in our work by allowing us to conduct observations in their homes.
- The A.L. Mailman Family Foundation, Luba Lynch, Executive Director, and Betty Bardige, Chair, for funding the video-DVD training package, and especially for their faith in us and in the value of our work.

Thelma Harms, Debby Cryer, and Richard M. Clifford
Frank Porter Graham Child Development Institute
January, 2007

Introduction to the FCCERS–R

The *Family Child Care Environment Rating Scale–Revised Edition* (FCCERS–R) is a thorough revision of the original *Family Day Care Rating Scale* (FDCRS; Harms & Clifford, 1989). It is one of a series of four scales that share the same format and scoring system but vary considerably in requirements, because each scale assesses a different age group and/or type of child care and education setting. The FCCERS–R retains the original broad definition of environment, including organization of space, interaction, activities, schedule, and provisions for parents and provider. The 38 items are organized into seven subscales: Space and Furnishings, Personal Care Routines, Listening and Talking, Activities, Interaction, Program Structure, and Parents and Provider. Since family child care homes frequently enroll a wide age range of children, this scale is designed to assess programs serving children from birth through school-agers, up to 12 years of age, including the provider's own children if present. Therefore, the FCCERS–R contains items to assess provisions in the environment for a wide age range, and to ensure protection of children's health and safety, appropriate stimulation through language and activities, and warm, supportive interaction.

Family child care providers often tell us that their program is "good" because the children they care for are treated just as their own children would be. But this point does not necessarily ensure the positive development we want for every child. In fact, it is challenging for any parent to meet the developmental needs of even one child to maximize positive development. In family child care, where a provider must meet the needs of a group of similarly aged children, or of a group of children who differ substantially in ages and abilities, the challenges multiply exponentially. A comprehensive, reliable, and valid instrument that assesses program quality and quantifies what is observed to be happening in a family child care home can play an important role in improving the quality of the care and educational experiences received by the children.

In order to define and measure quality, the FCCERS–R draws from three main sources: research evidence from a number of relevant fields (health, development, and education), professional views of best practice, and the practical constraints of real life in a family child care setting. The requirements of the FCCERS–R are based on what these sources judge to be important conditions for positive outcomes in children both while they are in the program and long afterward. The guiding principle here, as in all of our environment rating scales, has been to focus on what we know to be good for children.

Process of Revision

The process of revision drew on four main sources of information: (1) research on development in the infant, toddler, preschool, and school-age years and findings related to the impact of child care environments on children's health and development; (2) a content comparison of the original FDCRS with other assessment instruments designed for similar age groups and settings, and additional documents describing aspects of family child care program quality; (3) feedback from FDCRS users, solicited through a questionnaire that was circulated and also put on our website, as well as suggestions given to us as we talked with the many people who use the FDCRS; and (4) intensive use over the years, and across states and countries, by the FCCERS–R co-authors and their team of associates at the Frank Porter Graham Child Development Institute, University of North Carolina at Chapel Hill.

The data from studies of family child care program quality using the FDCRS gave us information about the range of scores on various items, the relative difficulty of items, and their validity. The content comparison helped us to identify items to consider for addition or deletion. By far the most helpful guidance for the revision was the feedback from direct use in the field. Colleagues from the United States, Canada, and Europe who had used the FDCRS in research, monitoring, and program improvement gave us valuable suggestions based on their experience with the scale. Using input from focus groups that were convened during the revisions of the *Early Childhood Environment Rating Scale* (ECERS) and *Infant/Toddler Environment Rating Scale* (ITERS), we were able to consider what was needed to make the revised FCCERS–R more sensitive to issues of inclusion and diversity.

Changes in the FCCERS–R

While retaining basic similarities in format and content that provide continuity between the FDCRS and FCCERS–R, the following changes were made to bring the scale in line with the other revised editions in the Environment Rating Scale (ERS) series:

1. The title of the scale was changed to represent the current term for this type of care. Instead of "family day care," the term *family child care* is used.
2. The indicators under each level of quality in an item were numbered so that they could be given a score of "Yes," "No," or "Not Applicable" (NA) on the scoresheet. This makes it possible to be more exact in reflecting observed strengths and weaknesses in an item.
3. Each item is printed on a separate page, followed by the Notes for Clarification.
4. Sample questions are included for indicators that are difficult to observe.
5. Negative indicators on the minimal level were removed and are now found only in the 1 (inadequate) level. In levels 3 (minimal), 5 (good), and 7 (excellent) only indicators of positive attributes are listed.
6. The Notes for Clarification have been expanded to give additional information to improve accuracy in scoring and to explain the intent of specific items and indicators.
7. Indicators and examples were added throughout the scale to make the items more inclusive. The subscale "FDCRS Supplementary Items: Provisions for Exceptional Children" was dropped. This follows the advice given to us by scale users to include indicators and examples in the scale instead of adding a separate subscale for children with disabilities.
8. Indicators and items were rewritten to be more culturally sensitive. The observer must note, however, that indicators for quality hold true across a diversity of cultures and individuals, although the ways in which they are expressed may differ. Whatever the personal styles of the provider being observed, the requirements of the indicators must be met, although there can be some variation in the way this is done.
9. Items that had two parts, "a" for infants/toddlers and "b" for older children were dropped, and new items were constructed to meet the needs of all age groups.
10. Items were added to or removed from all subscales including the following:
    - Space and Furnishings: Item 1. Indoor space used for child care was added, and Item 6. Space for privacy replaced FDCRS Item 6 a and b. Space to be alone.
    - Personal Care Routines: Item 11. Health practices was added, and FDCRS Item 11, Personal grooming was removed.
    - Listening and Talking: Items 13. Helping children understand language, and 14. Helping children use language were completely revised. Item 15. Using books was added. FDCRS items removed included 14 a. & b. Informal use of language, and 17. Helping children reason (using concepts).
    - Activities: Items 21. Math/number and 22. Nature/science were added.
    - Interaction subscale replaced FDCRS Social Development subscale, with revised FDCRS Item 26, now Item 27. Supervision of play and learning. The FDCRS Item 27. Tone was replaced with revised Item 28. Provider-child interaction, and Item 30. Interactions among children.
    - Program Structure subscale was added, and contains a revised FDCRS Item 25, now Item 31. Schedule and new Items 32. Free play and 33. Group time.
    - Parents and Provider: New Item 38. Provisions for professional needs was added.
11. Many remaining FDCRS items were changed significantly, including Helping children use language, Art, Use of TV, video, and/or computer, Schedule, Adaptations for special needs, and Relationships with parents.
12. The scaling of some of the items in the subscale Personal Care Routines was made more gradual to better reflect varying levels of health practices in real life situations.

Reliability and Validity

The FCCERS–R is part of a series of instruments widely used to assess quality in early childhood environments, based originally on the *Early Childhood Environment Rating Scale* (Harms & Clifford, 1980). In more than 30 years of use, research has shown that these instruments can be used reliably and consistently across a wide variety of settings and cultures (Clifford & Rossbach, 2004). They have been shown to provide quite stable results, yet are sensitive to organized attempts to improve early childhood environments (Bryant et al., 2003; Clifford & Rossbach, 2004). A number of studies have shown that environmental quality as defined by these instruments is predictive of child outcomes both during the period of time children are in these environments and as they move into school (Burchinal, Roberts, Nabors, & Bryant, 1996; Burchinal et al., 2000; Helburn, 1995; Peisner-Feinberg et al., 2001).

With the development of the substantially revised FCCERS–R, the authors relied heavily on work with the other scales, particularly with the recent revisions of the ECERS–R and ITERS–R instruments. Thus, while the revisions are substantial, they are based on the successful experiences with the other scales in the series. Given this situation, the primary goal of the field test of the FCCERS–R was to determine the extent to which the revised version of the family child care scale could be used reliably and meaningfully in real-life family child care settings. That is, we examined whether different observers using the scale in the same family child care setting at the same time get essentially the same results and whether these results are stable enough over time to ensure that what is being measured does not vary widely from day to day.

To accomplish this task, a two-phase field test was completed between March and November of 2006. The goal of the first phase of the field test was to establish the interrater reliability and other psychometric properties of the FCCERS–R. The second part of the field test sought to establish test-retest reliability.

In phase one, eight data collectors completed a half day of intensive training conducted by the instrument authors. These data collectors were all familiar with the ECERS-R and/or ITERS-R, so the training focused on the specifics of the new version of the family child care scale and the methods for collecting data in a family child care setting.

The trained observers conducted paired observations of 45 family child care homes. Each observer scored the items independently. Each observation lasted nearly 3 hours (Mean = 2 hours, 41 minutes; SD = 44 minutes), with an additional short interview lasting approximately 30 minutes (Mean = 30 minutes, SD = 13 minutes) with the caregiver.

The second part of the field test sought to establish test-retest reliability. A subgroup of 20 of the original family child care homes was selected for a second observation by one of the original observers in that setting approximately 14 weeks (Mean = 14.44, SD = 7.41; Minimum = 3.86; Maximum = 26.00) after the first observation.

Participants

Using the North Carolina Division of Child Development listing of family child care homes, an unbiased stratified sample of homes was selected for participation in field testing. The homes were from six counties in central North Carolina in the Research Triangle and Piedmont Triad areas of the state. These counties were chosen to provide a range of urban and rural settings. Programs in which English was not the primary language spoken by the family child care provider were excluded from the sample.

In order to document the ability of the FCCERS–R to reliably measure quality in settings with children of varying ages, and in both high and low quality settings, we selected a diverse sample of family child care providers for the field test.

The sample was stratified by the ages of children served, including those serving only infants and toddlers, those serving preschoolers and school-aged children, and those serving a wide range of ages in the program. While we had difficulty obtaining sufficient numbers of providers meeting these criteria during the short time frame of the study, we did get a very diverse population of family child care programs in the final sample.

In the final sample 47% (21 homes) of the family child care homes had at least one child under the age of 1, 27% (12 homes) had only children under the age of 3 enrolled, and 7% (3 homes) of the homes enrolled only children who were over 2½ years old. In the 20 family child care homes that were part of the retest, 47% of the homes had at least one child under the age of 1, 50% had only children under the age of 3 enrolled, and approximately 8% of the homes enrolled only children who were over 2½ years old. Thus we met our goal of including a broad range of age groupings in our field test samples.

Our sample was also stratified to reflect the broad range of quality typically found in family child care homes. North Carolina uses a star rating system to provide families with a guide to quality in the family child care homes in the state, with a one-star family child care home meeting only the basic licensing requirements. Programs with two to five stars meet increasingly difficult requirements. Our sampling process sought to obtain approximately one-third of the programs for the study from one- or two-star ratings, one-third with a three-star rating, and one-third with a four- or five-star rating.

In the final sample approximately 24% (11 homes) of the family child care homes had a one- or two-star rating, 20% (9 homes) had a three-star rating, and approximately 56% (25 homes) had a four- or five-star rating. Among the 20 family child care homes that participated in the retest, 40% (8 homes) had a one- or two-star rating, 10% (2 homes) had a three-star rating, and 50% (10 homes) had a four- or five-star rating. Overall, the homes used as part of our sample had a wide range of quality ratings as indicated by the star rating system in North Carolina. In the final sample all levels of rated licenses are represented, and all age ranges served in family child care are represented.

Statistical Procedures

Using SAS and Microsoft Excel, a variety of statistical procedures were used to measure the psychometric properties of the FCCERS–R. As described previously, the scale is made up of some 460 separate indicators arranged into 38 items that are grouped into 7 subscales and finally given an overall score. Items are given equal weighting for determining both the subscale scores and the total score, so these scores are simply the average of all items scored in each subscale and the average of all items scored in the entire scale, respectively. Results of our analyses at each of these levels are discussed below.

Indicator Reliability. Each indicator is given a simple "yes" or "no" score, with a "not applicable" possible for a few of the indicators. Thus indicator agreement is simply the percentage of time that the two observers rate the indicator the same way. The mean percent agreement for all ratings in which both observers gave a score to the indicator was 88.5%.

Item Reliability. As described previously, indicators are grouped into items, with each item having a possible score of 1–7. Reliability at the item level is measured in several ways. First the simple percentage of times the two observers scored an item within one point of one another is shown. As shown in Table 1, only one item had reliability scores below 80% within one point, and the average across all items was 88.44%.

A more sophisticated measure of reliability known as Cohen's kappa (Cohen, 1960) is used to correct for both the distribution of scores given in the study, and the amount of difference between the scores given by each observer. We used the weighted kappa version of the statistic for these analyses. In the weighted kappa, when all of the scores in a study tend to be grouped closely together, observers whose scores are far from the others are penalized heavily. Additionally, the weighted kappa accounts for the degree of difference between the two observers' scores. That is, an observation in which one observer scores a 1 and the other scores a 7 is given a lower kappa than if one scores a 1 and the other a 2.

Table 1. Item Reliability for the FCCERS–R

Item	Number of Homes Scored	Mean Score	Mean Percentage Within 1	Weighted Kappa
1. Indoor Space	45	4.00	88.89 %	0.74
2. Furniture	45	3.23	82.22 %	0.71
3. Provision for Comfort	45	3.17	95.56 %	0.75
4. Arrangement of Space	45	1.96	86.67 %	0.53
5. Display for Children	45	2.96	88.89 %	0.69
6. Space for Privacy	45	2.41	88.89 %	0.63
7. Greeting/Departing	45	4.72	82.22 %	0.69
8. Nap/Rest	45	1.74	91.11 %	0.56
9. Meals/Snacks	45	1.43	91.11 %	0.37
10. Diapering/Toileting	45	1.48	95.56 %	0.49
11. Health Practices	45	2.07	86.67 %	0.47
12. Safety Practices	45	1.27	97.78 %	0.46
13. Helping Understand Language	45	3.74	82.22 %	0.59
14. Helping Children Use Language	45	3.52	86.67 %	0.68
15. Using Books	45	2.34	93.33 %	0.71
16. Fine Motor	45	2.18	80.00 %	0.48
17. Art	45	2.77	91.11 %	0.68
18. Music and Movement	45	2.68	95.56 %	0.72
19. Blocks	45	2.19	80.00 %	0.43
20. Dramatic Play	45	3.01	82.22 %	0.73
21. Math/Number	45	2.20	88.89 %	0.48
22. Nature/Science	45	2.41	82.22 %	0.66
23. Sand and Water	45	3.88	84.44 %	0.70
24. Promoting Diversity	45	2.99	97.78 %	0.72
25. TV, Video, Computer	38	1.99	89.47 %	0.71
26. Active Physical Play	45	1.63	95.56 %	0.72
27. Supervision	45	3.09	80.00 %	0.63
28. Provider-Child Interaction	45	3.97	75.56 %	0.59
29. Discipline	45	3.36	82.22 %	0.65
30. Interactions Among Children	44	4.06	84.09 %	0.56
31. Schedule	45	2.70	93.33 %	0.81
32. Free Play	45	2.78	91.11 %	0.74
33. Group Time	37	3.86	81.08 %	0.60
34. Children with Disabilities	4	2.75	100.00 %	1.00
35. Provisions for Parents	45	5.09	95.56 %	0.82
36. Balance Personal/Care	45	4.73	80.00 %	0.66
37. Opportunities for Growth	45	5.41	95.56 %	0.85
38. Professional Needs	45	6.01	91.11 %	0.73

The more demanding weighted kappa measure revealed a few items with kappas below the standard of .60 that is generally accepted. As can be seen in Table 1, the items for which the weighted kappa was low were ones that tended to have very low scores. The weighted kappa statistic penalizes any variation in scores very heavily in such cases, resulting in the low scores shown in the table. However, we are convinced that these low average scores are an accurate reflection of practice in the United States and chose not to revise the items to get more variability and higher weighted kappa scores.

Subscale and Total Scale Reliability. As stated above, the reliability across all items was quite high at 88.44% within one point. Table 2 shows the mean percent agreement within one for each of the subscales and the total scale. As can be seen in the table, the percent agreement within one point ranged from just over 80% to just over 90% for the seven subscales. The mean kappas for the subscales, ranging from 0.62 to 0.77, were well within accepted standards. The mean weighted kappa for all items across all observers was a very respectable 0.71. In addition, we calculated the correlation between the two observers' scores for all settings. The correlation across all observations was 0.77. Clearly, observers using the FCCERS–R can achieve high levels of reliability with proper training and supervision.

Internal Consistency. The internal consistency of the subscales and full test was assessed using Cronbach's (1951) alpha, which is a measure of the degree to which the items in a scale or subscale appear to measure a similar concept. A Cronbach's alpha of 0.6 and higher is considered to indicate an acceptable level of internal consistency. The overall scale has a high level of internal consistency, with an alpha of 0.90 (see Table 3). Thus the total FCCERS–R score appears to be a measure of global quality that reflects a single major construct. While the overall FCCERS–R score meets the criteria, caution should be taken when interpreting the Personal Care Routines and the Parents and Provider subscales, as these subscales have a lower alpha, and so items within these subscales may be measuring different concepts. In general, we do not recommend using the subscale scores in research. However, the subscales are quite useful both for practitioners and for those providing technical assistance in the field.

Test-Retest Reliability. As described above, we also conducted a test-retest reliability assessment to examine the stability of the FCCERS–R measure-

Table 2. Subscale and Total Score Reliability

Subscale	Mean Percent Agreement Within 1	Mean Score	Weighted Kappa
Space and Furnishings	88.52 %	2.95	0.72
Personal Care Routines	90.74 %	2.12	0.69
Listening and Talking	87.41 %	3.21	0.69
Activities	87.91 %	2.55	0.68
Interaction	80.45 %	3.62	0.62
Program Structure	89.31 %	3.01	0.74
Parents and Provider	90.56 %	5.31	0.77
Full Scale	88.44 %	3.05	0.71

Table 3. Internal Consistency

Subscale	Alpha
Space and Furnishings	0.71
Personal Care Routines	0.46
Listening and Talking	0.83
Activities	0.88
Interaction	0.84
Program Structure	0.62
Parents and Provider	0.39
Full Scale	0.90

ment over time. In the 20 sites observed a second time, the original overall mean score was 3.32, and the mean in the second set of assessments was 3.39. Across all items in the two observations, the retest agreement within one point was 80.80% and the correlation between the test and retest assessments across all 20 sites was 0.73.

These results are certainly acceptable and fit with our assessors' informal reports. The assessors found that it was not unusual to find a different mixture of ages of children, different materials, and different arrangement of space in the sites from the original observation to the second observation. Such changes are to be expected in family child care over the relatively long period of time between assessments (14.44 weeks on average). These variations are random, so the very similar overall mean scores are to be expected. The test-retest agreement of about 80% within one point reflects the changes reported by our assessors while still being in a very respectable range of reliability.

Conclusion. It is clear from these results that the *Family Child Care Environment Rating Scale, Revised Edition* can be used in a reliable manner with trained and carefully supervised assessors. The item and overall levels of agreement are all well within accepted ranges for instruments of this type. The instrument displays a level of internal consistency associated with a single major construct, and most of the subscales show similarly high levels of internal consistency. The test-retest assessment demonstrates a reasonable level of stability over a substantial period of time, indicating that the assessment measures the more enduring aspects of quality that would not be expected to change radically from day to day. With careful training and supervision of observers, the new version of the rating scale is ideal for use in a wide range of applications, including research, regulation, training, technical assistance, and professional development, as well as by family child care practitioners for program improvement.

References

American Academy of Pediatrics, American Public Health Association, and National Resource Center for Health and Safety in Child Care. (2002). *Caring for Our Children: The National Health and Safety Performance Standards for Out-of-Home Child Care, 2ⁿᵈ edition.* Elk Grove Village, IL: American Academy of Pediatrics.

American Society for Testing and Materials International. (2006). *Annual Book of ASTM Standards.* Retrieved December 1, 2006, from http://www.astm.org

Bryant, D., Maxwell, K., Taylor, K., Poe, M., Peisner-Feinberg, E., & Bernier, K. (2003). *Smart Start and Preschool Child Care Quality in NC: Change Over Time and Relation to Children's Readiness.* Chapel Hill, NC: FPG Child Development Institute.

Burchinal, M., Roberts, J., Nabors, L., & Bryant, D. (1996). Quality of center child care and infant cognitive and language development. *Child Development, 67,* 606–620.

Burchinal, M., Roberts, J., Riggins, R., Jr., Ziesel, S. A., Neebe, E., & Bryant, D. (2000). Relating quality of center-based child care to early cognitive and language development longitudinally. *Child Development, 71,* 339–357.

Clifford, R. M., (2004, September/October), *Structure and Stability of the Early Childhood Environment Rating Scale.* Keynote Address at the Quality in Early Childhood Care and Education International Conference, Dublin, Ireland.

Clifford, R. M., & Rossbach, H. G. (2004). *Structure and Stability of the Early Childhood Environment Rating Scale.* In H. Schoenfeld, S. O'Brien, & T. Walsh (Eds.), *Questions of Quality* (pp. 12–21). Drumcondra, Dublin, Ireland: The Centre for Early Childhood Development and Education, The Gate Lodge, St. Patrick's College.

Cohen, J. (1960). A coefficient of agreement for nominal scales. *Educational and Psychological Measurement, 20,* 37–46.

Cronbach, L. J. (1951). Coefficient alpha and the internal structure of tests. *Psychometrika, 16,* 297–334.

Galinsky, E., Howes, C., Kontos, S., & Shinn, M. (1994). *The Study of Children in Family Child Care and Relative Care: Highlights of Findings.* New York: Families and Work Institute. (ERIC Document Reproduction Service No. ED388402).

Harms, T., & Clifford, R. M. (1980). *Early Childhood Environment Rating Scale.* New York: Teachers College Press.

Harms, T., & Clifford, R. M. (1989). *Family Day Care Rating Scale.* New York: Teachers College Press.

Harms, T., Clifford, R. M., & Cryer, D. (2005). *Early Childhood Environment Rating Scale* (Rev. ed.). New York: Teachers College Press.

Harms, T., Cryer, D., & Clifford, R. M. (2006). *Infant/Toddler Environment Rating Scale* (Rev. ed.). New York: Teachers College Press.

Helburn, S. (Ed.). (1995). *Cost, Quality, and Child Outcomes in Child Care Centers: Technical Report.* Denver: University of Colorado, Department of Economics, Center for Research in Economic Social Policy.

Microsoft Office Excel. (2003). [Computer software]. Redmond, WA: Microsoft Corporation.

National Association for Family Child Care. (2005). *Quality Standards for NAFCC Accreditation* (4ᵗʰ ed.). St. Paul, MN: Redleaf Press.

Peisner-Feinberg, E. S., Burchinal, M. R., Clifford, R. M., Culkin, M. L., Howes, C., Kagan, S. L., & Yazejian, N. (2001). The relation of preschool child-care quality to children's cognitive and social developmental trajectories through second grade. *Child Development, 72,* 1534–1553.

SAS for Windows. (2003). (Version 9.1). [Computer software]. Cary, NC: SAS Institute, Inc.

U.S. Consumer Product Safety Commission. (2006). *Handbook for Public Playground Safety* (No. 325). Washington, DC: U.S. Consumer Product Safety Commission.

Instructions for Using the FCCERS–R

It is important to be accurate in using the FCCERS–R whether you use the scale in your own home for self-assessment or as an outside observer for program monitoring, program evaluation, program improvement, or research. A video training package for the FCCERS–R is available from Teachers College Press for use in self-instruction or as part of group training. It is preferable to participate in a training sequence led by an experienced FCCERS–R trainer before using the scale formally. The training sequence for observers who will use the scale for monitoring, evaluation, or research should include at least two practice classroom observations with a small group of observers led by an experienced group leader, followed by an inter-rater agreement comparison. Additional field practice observations may be needed to reach the desired level of agreement, or to develop reliability within a group. Anyone who plans to use the scale should read the following instructions carefully before attempting to rate a program.

Administration of the Scale

1. The scale is designed to be used with one family child care home at a time, for children from birth through elementary school. If the family child care home is broken into separate groups with different providers and children rarely come together, a separate observation is required for each group. A block of at least 3 hours should be set aside for observation and rating if you are an outside observer, that is, anyone who is not part of the family child care home (e.g., technical assistance providers, consultants, licensing personnel, and researchers). Since scores based on provider report are less reliable than scores based on observation, it is essential to observe as many of the indicators as possible. Rely on provider report only for the relatively few indicators that cannot be observed.

2. A valid observation requires the presence of a representative sample of the children enrolled. It is recommended that during the observation preschoolers and infant/toddlers be present if children from those age group are enrolled, and that at least three-quarters of the children allowed to attend at any one time are present. Before you begin your observation, tell the provider exactly what you will be doing–completing the scale, following the family child care home's regular activities and routines to see what happens, looking at materials and areas the children use, going outside if the children do. Then ask the provider a few questions to complete the identifying information on the top of the first page of the Score Sheet. You will need to ask for some of the information, especially the birth dates of the oldest and youngest children, number of children enrolled in the group, and whether there are children with identified disabilities in the group. By the end of the observation, make sure all identifying information requested on the first page is complete. Also ask the provider to tell you which spaces are used for the program and which are not.

3. Arrange with the provider a time after your observation when you can ask questions about indicators you were not able to observe. It is best to set this time before arriving at the observation site, so that providers can free themselves from child care responsibilities while talking with you. Approximately 20–30 minutes will be required for questions.

4. Take a few minutes at the beginning of your observation to orient yourself to the home.
   - You may want to start with Items 1–6 in Space and Furnishings because some of the indicators are easy to observe and typically do not change during the observation.
   - Some items require observation of events and activities that occur only at specific times of the day (i.e., Items 7–10 in Personal Care Routines, Item 26. Active physical play). Be aware of those items so that you can observe and rate them as they occur.
   - Score items that assess aspects of relationships only after you have observed for a sufficient time to get a representative picture (i.e., Items 13–14 on language, Items 27–30 on interactions).
   - Item 15. Using books, and Items 16–26 in the Activities subscale will require both inspection of materials and observation of use of materials.

5. Be careful not to disrupt the ongoing activities while you are observing.
   - Maintain a pleasant but neutral facial expression.
   - Do not attract the children's interest or interact with them, unless you must stop something significantly endangering to a child and the provider is unable to handle the situation.
   - Do not talk to or interrupt the provider.
   - Be careful about where you place yourself to avoid disrupting the environment.
   - Remember that you are a guest in the provider's home. Be sure that you have the provider's permission before looking in any closed spaces,

sitting on furniture, or using his or her supplies. Such permission can be obtained before the observation begins.

6. In order to make the best use of the time set aside for asking questions:
   - Place a question mark on your Score Sheet next to any indicator that requires a question.
   - Use the sample questions provided, whenever applicable.
   - If you have to ask questions about items for which no sample questions have been provided, note your questions on the Score Sheet or another sheet of paper before talking with the provider.
   - Ask only those questions needed to decide whether a higher score is possible.
   - Ask questions on one item at a time, following the order of the items in the scale, and take notes or decide on a score before you move on to the next item.

7. Note that the Score Sheet, starting on page 69, provides a convenient way to record the ratings for indicators, items, subscales, and total scores, as well as your comments. The Profile that follows the Score Sheet permits a graphic representation of this information.
   - A fresh copy of the Score Sheet is needed for each observation. Permission is hereby given to photocopy the Score Sheet and Profile only, not the entire scale.
   - Ratings should be recorded on the Score Sheet before leaving the program. The observer should not leave the home until all ratings are completed, in case additional observed information is needed to score an item. Ratings should not be entrusted to memory for later recording.
   - Complete an assessment, including any report that is required, before doing another observation.
   - It is advisable to use a pencil with a good eraser on the Score Sheet during the observation, so that changes can be made easily.

Scoring System

1. Read the entire scale carefully, including the Items, Notes for Clarification, and Questions. In order to be accurate, all ratings must be based as exactly as possible on the indicators provided in the scale items.
2. The scale should be kept readily available and read constantly during the entire observation to make sure that the scores are assigned accurately.

3. Examples that differ from those given in the indicator but meet the intent of the indicator may be used as a basis for giving credit for an indicator.
4. Scores should be based on the current situation that is observed or reported by the provider. Scores should not be based on observer assumption or on the provider's future plans. In the absence of observable information on which to base your rating, you may ask questions of the provider during the interview after the observation and base scoring decisions on what is reported.
5. Requirements in the scale apply to *all* children in the group being observed, unless an exception is noted in an item.
6. When scoring an item, always start reading from 1 (inadequate) and progress upward till the correct quality score is reached.
7. Yes (Y) is marked on the scoresheet if the indicator is *true* for the situation being observed. No (N) is marked on the scoresheet if the indicator is *not true*. (For each numbered indicator, ask yourself, "Is this true, Yes or No?").
8. Ratings are to be assigned in the following way:
   - A rating of 1 must be given if *any* indicator under 1 is scored Yes.
   - A rating of 2 is given when all indicators under 1 are scored No and at least half of the indicators under 3 are scored Yes.
   - A rating of 3 is given when all indicators under 1 are scored No and all indicators under 3 are scored Yes.
   - A rating of 4 is given when all requirements of 3 are met and at least half of the indicators under 5 are scored Yes.
   - A rating of 5 is given when all requirements of 3 are met and all indicators under 5 are scored Yes.
   - A rating of 6 is given when all requirements of 5 are met and at least half of the indicators under 7 are scored Yes.
   - A rating of 7 is given when all requirements of 5 are met and all indicators under 7 are scored Yes.
   - A score of NA (not applicable) may only be given for indicators or for entire items when "NA permitted" is shown on the scale and there is an NA on the Score Sheet. Indicators that are scored NA are not counted when determining the rating for an item, and items scored NA are not counted when calculating subscale and total scale scores.
   - To calculate average subscale scores, sum the scores for each item in the subscale and divide by the number of items scored. The total mean scale score is the sum of all item scores for the entire scale divided by the number of items scored.

Alternate Scoring Option

Since each one of the indicators in the FCCERS–R can be given a rating, it is possible to continue to rate the indicators beyond the quality level score assigned to an item. Using the scoring system described above, indicators are typically rated only until an item quality score is assigned. However, if it is desirable, for purposes of research or program improvement, to gain additional information on areas of strength beyond the item quality level score, the observer can continue to rate all the indicators in an item.

If the alternate scoring option is selected and all indicators are scored, the required observation time and the questioning time will need to be extended considerably. An observation of approximately 3½–4 hours and a questioning time of approximately 45 minutes will be required to complete all indicators. The additional information may, however, be helpful in making plans for specific improvements and in the interpretation of research findings.

The Score Sheet and the Profile

The Score Sheet provides for both indicator and item scores. The indicator scores are Y (Yes), N (No), and NA (not applicable), which is permitted only as noted for selected indicators. The item quality scores are 1 (Inadequate) through 7 (Excellent), and NA (not applicable), which is permitted only as noted for selected items. There is also space provided for notes and sometimes forms to keep exact counts of specific information to justify the scores. Since notes are particularly helpful in counseling staff for improvement, we suggest taking more extensive notes on another sheet of paper for this purpose.

Care should be taken to mark the correct box under Y, N, or NA for each indicator. The numerical item quality score should be circled clearly.

The Profile permits a graphic representation of the scores for all items and subscales. It can be used to compare areas of strength and weakness, and to select items and subscales to target for improvement. There is also space for the mean subscale scores. The profiles for two observations can be plotted side by side to present changes visually.

Explanation of Terms Used Throughout the Scale

Accessible: Children can reach and are allowed to use toys, materials, furnishings, and/or equipment. Toys in open storage such as open shelves must be within easy reach of children. No barriers (verbal, such as a "no-touch" rule, or physical, such as being stored out of sight) can be present to prevent children from reaching them. For example, toys are not accessible if they are in containers with lids that the children cannot manage, unless the provider shows signs of regularly making the toys accessible to the children by opening various containers during the observation. If materials are stored out of reach, they must be placed within children's reach to be counted as accessible. For example, if they are stored in a closet, they must be brought out and placed where children can reach and use them. If stored out of a non-mobile child's reach, the child must be moved to reach the materials, or the materials must be placed close to the non-mobile child, within reach.

During an observation, if there is evidence that the provider regularly provides access to the variety of toys required for an item or indicator, credit can be given for "accessible." When the provider reports that particular materials are brought out for the children to use, but this was not observed, those materials must be shown to be easily accessible to the provider to give credit. Materials stored far from the child care space or crowded together so they are difficult to reach are not considered easily accessible to the provider. The observer should be sure to ask to see those materials that the provider reports using with the children, that were not accessible to children during the observation.

In a full-day program (operating 8 hours or more), unless stated in the item, materials must be accessible for at least 1 hour to give credit at the minimal level. Less time is required for programs operating for less than 8 hours. The required amount of time is calculated proportionally, based on the ratio of 1 hour for programs of 8 hours or more. Use the following chart to determine the approximate amount of time required for part-day programs.

Number of hours in operation	2 hrs.	3hrs.	4hrs.	5hrs.	6hrs.	7hrs.
Approximate minutes required for accessibility	15	25	30	40	45	50

Appropriate: Used in various items to mean age- and/or developmentally-suited for the children in the group being observed. In determining whether the requirements for "appropriate" are being met within the context of a particular indicator, the observer should consider whether the children's needs for protection of health and safety, stimulation, and positive relationships are being met in ways that are supportive and meaningful. "Appropriate" means challenging but not frustrating, in good working order so the material can be used for the designed purpose, and providing positive social messages, with no violent, frightening, prejudiced, or sexually explicit content.

Children. Includes all children enrolled who are 12 years of age or younger, including the provider's own children, children who are relatives of the provider, and children from unrelated families. Children within this age range who are "just visiting" must be included.

Daily. Every day, or almost every day, with very few unusual exceptions.

Handwashing: For children, including infants, and staff, hands must be washed with soap and warm running water for about 10 seconds. Hands must be dried with individual towels that are not shared (or air-dried with a blower). Using wipes or antiseptic waterless washes cannot be substituted for handwashing, since these do not effectively get rid of germs. However, for *very young infants* who have little body or head control, use of a disposable wipe is an acceptable substitute. Use of gloves does not eliminate the need for providers to wash their hands thoroughly whenever needed. See item specific information on handwashing in the Notes for Clarification for Item 9. Meals/snacks, Item 10. Diapering/toileting, and Item 11. Health practices.

Infants, Toddlers, Preschoolers, School-agers: "Infants" are defined as children from birth through 11 months of age. "Toddlers" are children between the ages of 12 and 30 months. "Preschoolers" are children between the ages of 30 months through Kindergarten. "School-agers" are children who are in first grade and older.

The requirements for the different age groups vary by item. Apply the item requirements for each age group whenever an age group is enrolled in the home being observed.

In all items or indicators where a particular age cut-off is given (e.g., "Score NA when only children under 1 year of age are enrolled."), some flexibility is allowed. If there is only one child in the group who exceeds the age cut-off, and that child is *less than* one month older than the age requirement, then the item/indicator can still be marked NA. If the child is more than one month older than the age cut-off, or if there are two or more children who exceed the age cut-off, then the item/indicator must be scored.

An exception to this rule is applied when a child with a disability is enrolled. In this case, the necessity for a requirement will depend on the child's abilities and disabilities. For example, if a child has a speech/language disability, and does not have limited physical abilities, then many requirements would still apply, such as for certain furnishings or activities that are not speech/language related.

Much of the day: In most items, "much of the day" is associated with the children's access to materials typically used indoors (e.g., books, art materials, fine motor or dramatic play toys). It means most of the time that any child may be awake and able to play. If children are prevented from using materials for long periods by lengthy routines, being kept in groups, or being kept in areas where access is not possible, then credit cannot be given for "much of the day." Usually such materials are not required outdoors to give credit for "much of the day" because active physical play is of primary importance for outdoor times. However, if children are kept outdoors for extremely long periods (⅓ of the day or more), thus limiting access to materials typically used indoors, then to give credit for "much of the day," such materials must be provided outdoors as well. Appropriate group activities in which children are engaged and interested for short periods that match their abilities are permissible as long as they do not significantly affect access to materials throughout the day. For non-mobile infants, all required toys or materials do not have to be accessible at the same time during the whole observation because of problems with clutter. However, there must be clear indications that the required variety and numbers of materials are accessible at various times during the day.

Some and *many*: Used throughout the scale to denote quantity of materials, equipment, toys, etc. Specific guidelines may be given in various items. "Some" denotes presence of a material in the environment, and at least 1 example must be observed, unless the guidelines require more examples. To give credit for "many," children should have access to materials without long periods of waiting or undue competition. These terms are also used to denote frequency, especially in items that evaluate language and interactions. For these items, "some" means that the requirement is observed regularly, but not frequently, throughout the observation.

Provider: Generally refers to the adult who is directly involved with the children, caring for and educating them. In the scale, provider is used in the singular because there is usually only one adult working with the children in a family child care home. However, in some cases, for example in a family child care home with a larger group of children enrolled, more than one provider may be present. In this case, all providers should be considered when scoring. When individual providers handle things differently, it is necessary to arrive at a score that characterizes the overall impact of the providers on the children. For example, in a home where one staff member is very verbal and the other is relatively nonverbal, the score is determined by how well the children's need for verbal input is met.

In all items involving any type of interaction, "provider" refers to an adult (or adults) who is in the home and works with the children daily (or almost daily), for much of the day. This can include volunteers or relatives, if they are in the home for the required amount of time. Adults who are in the home for short periods of the day, or who are not a regular daily part of the program, do not count in evaluating whether the requirements of the item are met. For example, if the provider's teen-aged son, daughter, husband, or a child's parent participates in the program and interacts with the children for short or irregular periods, these interactions do not count in scoring *unless they have a substantial negative impact on the operation of the group, or on one or more specific children.* When a part-time provider regularly works in a home during specific periods of the day and is present on a daily basis, his or her interactions should be considered in scoring.

Supervision. In family child care, it is usually necessary for providers to leave children for short periods of time, for example to use the toilet, prepare food, answer the door or phone, etc. The provider is only allowed limited, momentary lapses in supervision (2–4 minutes), and when children are out of sight, they must be within hearing range. In addition, children must be in a safe place, involved in low-risk activities (eating is a high-risk activity) while not within view, and checked on frequently. Children under the age of 6 generally cannot be left outdoors unsupervised, and older children must be checked regularly. Flexibility is allowed in determining the amount of supervision children require, based on how safe the environment is, the ages of the children, and their abilities.

Usually: Used to indicate the common or prevalent practice observed, which is carried out with only a few lapses. In some items, "usually" means 75% of the time, and this is indicated in the Notes for Clarification of the item.

Weather permitting: The term "weather permitting" is used in several items of the scale with regard to when children can participate in outdoor activities. "Weather permitting" means *almost every day*, unless there is active precipitation, or public announcements that advise people to remain indoors due to weather conditions, such as high levels of pollution or extreme cold or heat that might cause health problems. It is sometimes said, "There is no bad weather; only bad clothes." Therefore, children should be dressed properly and taken outdoors on most days. This might require that the schedule be changed to allow children outdoor play in the early morning if it will be very hot later in the day. Or it might require that the program ensure that children have boots and a change of clothes for a day when the grass is wet. After bad weather, staff should check the outdoor area, dry off equipment, sweep away water, or block off puddles, as needed, before children go out. Programs with protected outdoor areas, such as a covered deck or patio, are more likely to be able to meet the requirements for allowing outdoor activity daily, weather permitting.

Overview of the Subscales and Items of the FCCERS-R

Inadequate		Minimal		Good		Excellent
1	2	3	4	5	6	7

SPACE AND FURNISHINGS

1. Indoor space used for child care

1.1 Not enough space used in the home for child care children, play materials, and furnishings.*

1.2 Space lacks adequate lighting, ventilation, temperature control, and sound-absorbing materials.

1.3 Space is in such poor repair that children are in danger or care is compromised (Ex. rough, damaged floors; plumbing problems; unfinished construction).*

1.4 Space is poorly maintained (Ex. accumulation of dirt and grime on floors and rugs; sinks dirty; daily cleaning neglected).

3.1 Enough space used in the home for child care children, play materials, and furnishings.*

3.2 Adequate lighting, ventilation, temperature control, and sound-absorbing materials.

3.3 Space is generally in good repair with no major problems that endanger children or compromise care.*

3.4 Space is reasonably clean and well-maintained.*

5.1 Ample indoor space for child care children, play materials, and furnishings (Ex. children and adults can move around freely; space allows many play materials to be accessible at same time; space for equipment needed by children with disabilities; spacious open area for children to play).*

5.2 Some direct natural lighting through windows, doors, or skylights.

5.3 Space for children is accessible to all children and adults with disabilities currently using child care space (Ex. ramps and handrails for people with disabilities; access for wheelchairs and walkers).* *NA permitted.*

7.1 Natural light and ventilation can be controlled as needed (Ex. adjustable blinds or curtains for nap area; windows can be opened; ventilating fan can be used in bathroom).*

7.2 Floors, walls, and other built-in surfaces made of easy-to-clean materials where needed (Ex. washable floors/floor covering in eating and messy play areas; counters and cabinets have easy-to-clean surfaces).

7.3 Space for children is accessible to children and adults with disabilities.*

(See Notes for Clarification and Questions on next page)

1.1, 3.1. Consider all indoor space that child care children are allowed to use and give more weight to spaces used for more time. Base space needs on the largest number of children allowed to attend the family child care home at one time, including the provider's own children if they are part of the child care group. Enough indoor space requires that children's routine care needs can be met, there is space for basic furniture, and some space is provided for children's play. Even though the indoor space is often shared with the family, the child care space needs must be adequately met. Do not count space that children are not allowed to use.

1.3, 3.3. These indicators refer to the space used by children, not to furnishings, equipment, or materials that are in the space.

3.4. It is expected that there will be some messiness from the regular activities of the day. "Reasonably clean" means that there is evidence of daily maintenance, such as floors being vacuumed and mopped, and that big messes, such as food on floor after children have been fed, are cleaned up promptly.

5.1. "Ample space" means that in most areas used for routines and play, children are not crowded. Consider all indoor space used during the whole day and give more weight to spaces used for more time. If 2 or more frequently used spaces do not allow free movement, score "No." All spaces do not need to be used at the same time.

5.3, 7.3. To give credit for accessibility, the home and all spaces used for child care must be accessible to individuals with disabilities. Doorways must be at least 32 inches wide. The door handles must be operated with limited use of hands. The entrance door threshold should be ½ inch high or less and, if over ¼ inch, must be beveled to make it easier to roll over. If there are other obvious impediments to access for individuals with disabilities (such as narrow doorway to toilet, stairs with no ramp or elevator), credit cannot be given. In order for the indoor space used by children to be considered minimally acceptable (5.3), it must be accessible to children and adults with disabilities who are currently a part of the program. For a score of 7, accessibility is required regardless of whether or not individuals with disabilities are involved in the program.

7.1. Doors to outside count as ventilation only if they can be left open without posing a safety threat (for example, if they have a locking screen door or safety gate to keep children from leaving the room unattended).

Questions

7.1. Can the ventilation in space used for child care be controlled? *If yes, ask:* How is this done?

Inadequate		Minimal		Good		Excellent
1	2	3	4	5	6	7

2. Furniture for routine care, play, and learning

1.1 Not enough furniture to meet needs of child care children for routine care: feeding, sleeping, diapering/toileting, storage of children's possessions and routine care supplies.*

1.2 Not enough furniture for play and learning.*

1.3 Furniture is generally in such poor repair that children could be injured (Ex. splinters or exposed nails; wobbly legs on chairs).

3.1 Enough furniture for routine care.*

3.2 Enough furniture for play and learning for all ages/abilities of children enrolled.*

3.3 All furniture is sturdy and in good repair.*

5.1 Most tables/chairs used for eating, play, and learning activities made suitable to children's size (Ex. cushions or booster seats used with adult chairs to prevent need for children to kneel).*

5.2 Furnishings well cared for (Ex. sheets changed weekly or more; tables washed and sanitized before and after eating or washed after art activity).

5.3 Furniture promotes self-help as needed (Ex. steps near sink; special chair for child with physical disability; low open shelves for accessible toy storage; special storage accessible only to school-agers).*

5.4 Some storage used for extra toys and supplies.

5.5 Some adult seating used in routine care.*

7.1 At least one child-sized table with chairs used for toddlers/older children.*
NA permitted.

7.2 Routine care furniture accessible and convenient (Ex. cots/mats easy for providers to access; place to store diapers/diapering supplies near diapering table; cubbies placed for easy use by parents, providers, and older children).*

7.3 Comfortable adult seating for working with children in routines and play.*

(See Notes for Clarification and Questions on next page)

16

1.1, 3.1. Since children of different ages and abilities have different needs for routine care furniture, each age group in care must have appropriate provisions. For example, infants need cribs for sleeping, while older children need cots, mats, or beds for naps. All children need individual provisions for storing their personal possessions. Preschoolers and older children need easy access to their storage space, while only parents and providers need easy access to storage used for possessions of infants and toddlers. Unless all children are fed at the same time, 1 chair per child is not required. Younger children in diapers need a diapering table or appropriate alternative diapering surface, such as a plastic mat.

1.2. Consider the needs of the age and abilities of the children enrolled. Examples of furniture for play and learning are: infant seats, tables and chairs for activities or homework, low open shelves or dishpans/baskets/milk crates for toy storage.

3.2. Sufficient easily accessible storage for play and learning materials is required to get credit for this indicator, without having materials crowded into a small space. Accessible storage that accommodates very few materials does not meet the requirement for this indicator. Non-mobile children do not necessarily require access to storage shelves as long as materials are brought to them.

3.3. Sturdiness is a property of the furniture itself (i.e., will not break, fall over, or collapse when used). If sturdy furniture is placed so that it can be easily knocked over, this is a problem with safety, not the sturdiness of the furniture. Don't be overly perfectionistic when scoring this indicator. If there is only a very minor problem that does not create a likely safety hazard, then give credit for this indicator. For example, if a chair or table is slightly wobbly, but will not collapse, or if a vinyl-covered couch is slightly worn, but foam is not exposed, then do not count off for these small things, unless there are a substantial number of small problems.

5.1. "Most" means that 75% of the table/chairs are made suitable to the children's size, if needed. If all tables and chairs used are child-sized, give credit.

5.3. To give credit, at least two different kinds of provisions must be observed during the observation (Ex. steps at sink, low open storage for toys).

5.5, 7.3. At least one instance of use must be observed. When a family child care home sets space aside only for child care use, some adult seating is needed in that space. Sometimes providers use preschool-sized chairs or other furniture (such as very large blocks or cubes) to sit on while feeding children who are in high chairs or at very low tables. Credit can be given if they seem to work well for the provider. However, credit for such make-shift arrangements cannot be given under 7, where comfortable adult-sized furniture is required.

7.1. To give credit, 75% of the table/chairs must be child-sized. Child-sized chairs allow children to sit back in the chair with feet touching the floor (not necessarily flat on the floor). Children should not have to perch on edge of the chair for feet to touch floor. A child-sized table allows children's knees to fit comfortably under the table while elbows rest on table surface. Do not consider high chairs or group feeding tables, that *toddlers* must be put into by an adult, to be child-sized. Be sure to consider tables/chairs used by school-agers if enrolled.

7.2. Routine care furniture must be easy to access when needed, but not necessarily in the same room. "Convenient" placement means that it is possible to meet children's routine care needs with minimal lapses in supervision, taking into consideration the age and abilities of the children.

7.3. Adult seating with back support should be provided next to child-sized furnishings for care and learning (e.g., meals, play activities) so helping adults do not strain their backs while assisting children. Adult-sized furniture must match the task being performed. A rocking chair is appropriate for feeding a baby, but not for supervising children at a child-sized table.

Questions

1.1. Where do the children sleep? What sleeping arrangements are used?

5.4. Do you use any other toys or materials in addition to what I observed? *If yes, ask:* Where are they stored? Could you please show me?

7.2. *If cots or mats are not visible during the observation, ask:* Where are the children's cots or mats stored?

Inadequate		Minimal		Good		Excellent
1	2	3	4	5	6	7

3. Provision for relaxation and comfort

1.1 No "softness" provided for children at play (Ex. no upholstered furniture, rug areas, cushions, or soft toys provided for play).*

3.1 Some rug or other soft furnishing accessible during play (Ex. large cushion, quilt on floor, couch, bean bag chair).*

3.2 Three or more soft toys accessible.*

5.1 Furnishings providing a substantial amount of softness are accessible much of the day.*

5.2 Children using soft furnishings for relaxation are protected from active play.*

5.3 Many soft toys accessible much of the day.*

7.1 Softness accessible in more than one area in child care space (Ex. couch in living room and bean bag chairs in play room, cozy area for reading, and child-sized couch in housekeeping corner).

7.2 Soft, child-sized furnishings provided especially for children (Ex. small upholstered chair or couch).*

7.3 Soft furnishings used for reading or other quiet play.*

---

*Notes for Clarification

1.1. Refers to softness provided other than that found in sleeping arrangements (cribs, cots, mats, beds) or other padded routine-care furnishings.

3.1, 5.1. Some use must be observed to give credit.

3.2. Examples of soft toys are: cloth or vinyl covered foam blocks, cloth dolls, stuffed toy animals, cloth puppets, and so forth. Do not count cloth or vinyl books as soft toys.

5.1. A thin mat, cushion, or a carpet alone would not meet this requirement. Typically, a substantial amount of softness includes a combination of soft furnishings, but a large single furnishing, such as a couch, mattress, or futon could meet the requirement, if it provides the substantial amount of softness needed by children.

5.2. Protection from active play can be provided physically by placing soft furnishings out of traffic and/or behind a barrier, or through supervision to ensure that active children do not interfere with the child who is relaxing. If children are observed using soft furnishings without interference, score "Yes." To give credit for 5.2 there must be a substantial amount of softness.

5.3. To meet the requirement of "many," there should be at least 10 soft toys, and at least 2 per child if there are more than 5 children.

7.2. Must be available for all ages of children enrolled.

7.3. To give credit, at least 1 instance must be observed during the observation.

Inadequate		Minimal		Good		Excellent
1	2	3	4	5	6	7

4. Arrangement of indoor space for child care

1.1 Arrangement of space leaves little room for routine care and play (Ex. baby must be diapered on living room rug or couch; space crowded with children's routine care furnishings or materials/ furnishings children are not allowed to use).

1.2 Arrangement of space makes it extremely difficult to adequately supervise children (Ex. young children allowed to use multiple rooms at the same time with one provider supervising; infants sleep in room where they are not within view; school-agers play in areas where they cannot be heard and easily checked on).*

1.3 Children inappropriately restricted in use of space (Ex. infants/toddlers kept in swings/cribs/playpens during most play time; children kept at tables for long periods).

3.1 Furnishings placed to provide some open uncrowded space for play.

3.2 Arrangement of space allows adequate supervision of children without major difficulties.*

3.3 Space cleared of breakable objects and things dangerous to children.*

3.4 Most spaces used for child care accessible to children with disabilities enrolled in the group. *NA permitted.*

5.1 Space is arranged so that routine care and play activities can be carried out to meet children's needs without major problems (Ex. toileting/diapering area close to play area; food preparation area permits easy supervision of children at play; traffic patterns do not interfere with play activities).

5.2 Space provided to allow different kinds of activities to go on at the same time (Ex. quiet and active play activities for younger and older children; protected space for homework or completing puzzle with many pieces).

5.3 Materials for different kinds of activities are usually organized by type for productive use by children (Ex. sets of blocks stored separately; books on book shelf or in a basket; dramatic play materials gathered in one place; different types of toys not mixed in toy box).

7.1 Materials are usually placed for easy access by children, conveniently close to enough space where they can be used without interference (Ex. rattle, soft toy, crawling areas for infants; books, fine motor, gross motor areas for toddlers; art, fine motor, blocks, dramatic play areas for preschoolers; homework, art, games for school-agers).*

7.2 Arrangement usually promotes independent use of furnishings and materials (Ex. steps placed near sink, low open shelves located in play area, picture labels used to guide clean-up).

7.3 Convenient, organized storage for extra toys and materials.

*Notes for Clarification

1.2, 3.2. See "supervision" in "Explanation of Terms Used Throughout the Scale" on page 11. In scoring consider the ages and abilities of children, as well as personal characteristics such as impulsivity. In general, the younger the child, or the more hazards present in the space, the greater the need for easy visual supervision.

3.3. In scoring, consider the relative severity of the hazards and the likelihood that serious injury could occur. Score "Yes" if no more than 3 hazards are observed.

7.1. Space and play surfaces should be suitable for the type of material being used. For example, blocks need a steady surface; scribbling requires a hard surface under the paper and room for children to move their arms freely. Infants require fewer, more flexible play areas, while toddlers and older children need a wider variety of play spaces.

Inadequate		Minimal		Good		Excellent
1	2	3	4	5	6	7

5. Display for children

1.1 No pictures or other materials displayed specifically for the child care children.

1.2 Inappropriate materials displayed where child care children can see them (Ex. frightening materials, materials showing violence, sexually explicit materials, negative stereotypes of any group).

3.1 At least 3 colorful pictures and/or other materials displayed where child care children can easily see them (Ex. mobiles, photos, posters).*

3.2 Content of display is generally appropriate (Ex. not frightening; showing things that are meaningful to children).

3.3 At least two pieces of work done by the children currently enrolled is displayed where it can be easily seen by the children (Ex. scribble pictures, drawings, paintings, written work).*
NA permitted.

5.1 Many colorful, simple pictures, posters, and/or photographs displayed throughout the space where children spend the majority of their time.*

5.2 Many items displayed where children can easily see them, some within easy reach.*

5.3 Much work done by the children is displayed.*

5.4 Provider talks to the children about displayed materials.*

7.1 Photographs of children in the group, their families, pets, or other familiar faces displayed on child's eye level.

7.2 Individualized children's work predominates.*

7.3 New materials added or display changed at least monthly.

---

*Notes for Clarification

3.1. When the only display is wallpaper with colorful pictures designed for children, or a mural painted on the wall, credit can be given for this indicator, but not for 5.1.

3.1, 5.2. Display does not necessarily have to be at the child's eye level to be easily seen. However, the display must be in the children's path of vision and large and clear enough to be easily understood. Observe the display, keeping the children's size, mobility level, and activity patterns in mind. Consider size (large or small) and clarity. For example, a small photograph, or a poster showing many small things would not be considered easily seen if displayed up high, but would if displayed at eye level.

3.3. Score NA when only children under 1 year of age are enrolled. Work by children under 1 year of age is not required. If unsure about who did the items displayed, ask the question provided for this indicator. A total of 2 pieces of work is required, not 2 for each child enrolled.

5.1. Do not consider children's artwork in scoring this indicator. Children's work is considered in 5.3.

5.2. "Many" does not require a specific number. Score based on the overall impact of what is displayed for children in the space(s) they use most frequently. Display is not required in all areas.

5.3. "Much" means at least 2 times the number of children over 12 months of age currently enrolled. For example, if there are 3 children over 12 months of age, then at least 6 pieces of their work is required. Display must include some work done by child care children who are not family members, if they are enrolled.

5.4. To give credit, at least 1 instance must be observed during the observation.

7.2. Individualized work means that each child has selected the subject and/or media and has carried out the work in his or her own creative way. Thus, individualized products look quite different from one another. Projects where children follow a provider's example and little creativity is allowed are not considered individualized work.

---

*Questions

3.3, 5.3. Please tell me who did the children's work that is displayed. Are they currently enrolled?

7.3. Do you add to or change what is displayed for children, such as the pictures on the wall? *If yes, ask:* About how often?

Inadequate		Minimal		Good		Excellent
1	2	3	4	5	6	7

6. Space for privacy*

1.1 Children not allowed to play alone or with a friend, protected from intrusion by other children.

1.2 Children isolated by provider inappropriately without interaction and/or something interesting to do for long periods (Ex. kept in infant seat or swing; toddler in playpen or high chair; child with disability not included in activities; lengthy time out for preschooler; school-ager required to do homework alone without interaction).*

3.1 Children are allowed to find or create space for privacy (Ex. behind furniture or room dividers, in outdoor play equipment, in a quiet corner of the room).

3.2 All spaces used for privacy can be easily supervised by provider.*

5.1 Space set aside for one or two children to play, protected from intrusion by others (Ex. puts baby into protected area while using popular toys; no-interruption rule; small space protected by shelves).*

5.2 Space set aside for privacy accessible for use for much of the day.

7.1 More than one space available for privacy.

7.2 Provider sets up activities for one or two children to use in private space.

---

*Notes for Clarification

Item 6. The intent of space for privacy is to give children relief from the pressures of group life. A place where one or two children can play protected from intrusion by other children, yet be supervised by the provider, is considered space for privacy. Private space can be created by using physical barriers such as book shelves; by enforcing the rule that children may not interrupt one another; by limiting the number of children working at a table placed in an out-of-traffic area. Examples of space for privacy are an activity where use is limited to one or two children: a cardboard box with large cut-out windows for easy supervision; a small outdoor play house; a table, easel, or computer limited to one or two children at a time. Score this item based on observation only, not provider report.

1.2. In order to judge whether the period of isolation is too long, look at the response of the child, for example if the child shows signs of boredom or unhappiness without the provider taking action to improve the situation.

3.2. Space for privacy for infants/toddlers and preschoolers must be easy to supervise visually whenever it is being used. Private space for school-agers must be located so provider can check on children frequently.

5.1. Provider must enforce the protection rule, if needed, in order to be given credit for this indicator. Space that is used only for punishment, for example time out, is not given credit. To give credit, the space must be observed.

Questions

7.2. Do you ever set up activities for just one or two children, away from the activities for the rest of the children? If so, please give examples.

Inadequate		Minimal		Good		Excellent
1	2	3	4	5	6	7

PERSONAL CARE ROUTINES

7. Greeting/departing*

1.1 Greeting of children is often neglected.

1.2 Departure is not safe or well-organized (Ex. child allowed to leave with unauthorized person; possessions difficult to find).

1.3 Parents rarely enter area used for child's care.*

3.1 Most children greeted warmly (Ex. provider seems pleased to see children; smiles; uses pleasant voice).*

3.2 Departure is safe and well-organized (Ex. child is released only to authorized person; children's things ready to go; diapers recently changed).

3.3 Parents enter caregiving area as part of daily greeting and departing routines.*

3.4 Some sharing of child-related information between parents and provider (Ex. medication needed; notified of illness in group; early pick-up; project school-ager is working on).

5.1 Provider greets each child individually and provides pleasant, organized departure (Ex. conversation on arrival; clothes ready for departure).

5.2 Problems with arrival/departure handled sensitively (Ex. provider comforts crying child during separation; allows child to play while talking to parent; listens to school-agers about their day at school).

5.3 Each parent greeted warmly.

5.4 Provider shares information about infant's routines with parents daily.
NA permitted.

7.1 Friendly, relaxed atmosphere that encourages parents to spend time visiting at drop-off and pick-up times (Ex. parent and provider chat while child gets settled; parent reads to child).

7.2 In addition to providing information about care routines/child's health/safety, provider talks to parents about specific things their child did during the day (Ex. play activities child enjoyed; new skill child worked on).

*Notes for Clarification

Item 7. At greeting and departure the responsibility for the child is transferred from one adult to another, therefore greeting requires that the child is acknowledged in some way immediately upon arrival or very shortly thereafter.

1.3, 3.3. Interpret "parents" as any adults who are responsible for the care of the child, such as grandparents, foster parents, or nannies. Parents of school-age children are required to enter caregiving area when bringing or picking up their children.

3.1. "Most" means 75% of the children.

Questions

If neither greeting nor departing are observed, ask: Can you describe what happens when children arrive and leave? *Follow up with more specific questions if needed, such as:*

1.3, 3.3. What do the parents usually do?

3.2, 5.1. What is done to prepare for children's leaving?

5.2. If a child has difficulty letting his or her parent leave or leaving at the end of the day, how is this handled?

7.1. Do parents ever spend time visiting at drop-off and pick-up times?

7.2. Is it possible for you to talk to parents at pick-up times? *If yes, ask:* What sort of things are discussed?

Inadequate		Minimal		Good		Excellent
1	2	3	4	5	6	7

8. Nap/rest*

1.1 Nap/rest schedule is inappropriate for most of the children (Ex. too early or too late; infants left in cribs for more than 15 minutes while happily awake or more than 2–3 minutes when unhappy; school-agers required to nap).

1.2 Provisions for nap/rest not healthful (Ex. crowded area; sleeping children disturbed; infants put to sleep on stomach; suffocation hazards in cribs).*

1.3 Little or no supervision provided or supervision is harsh (Ex. sleeping infant not within sight; children not checked while sleeping; provider not inside while children are napping).

3.1 Nap/rest is scheduled appropriately for each child (Ex. individual schedule for infants; toddlers eased into group schedule; older children allowed to rest for shorter time).

3.2 Healthful provisions for nap/rest (Ex. cribs/cots/mats not crowded; clean bedding for each child).*

3.3 Sufficient supervision provided for children during nap.*

5.1 Children are helped to relax (Ex. soft music; child soothed by patting back).

5.2 All cribs/cots/mats are 36 inches apart unless separated by a solid barrier.

5.3 Supervision is pleasant, responsive, and warm.*

7.1 Nap is personalized (Ex. crib/cot placed in same place; familiar practices; special blanket or cuddly toy for toddlers).

7.2 Activities provided for children who are not sleeping (Ex. early risers and non-nappers have quiet activities; infants taken out of cribs to play).

*Notes for Clarification

Item 8. All programs, no matter how long or short, should have individual provisions for infants, toddlers, and preschoolers to nap or rest and also for school-agers if they are tired. For programs of less than 4 hours in length, where nap is not a regular part of the day and the children do not seem tired, this item may be marked NA.

1.2, 3.2. To give credit for appropriate and healthful provisions, sleeping children should use their own crib/cot/mat. Linens, such as sheets, blankets, or sleeping bags, should be washed weekly or more often if needed. Children should not sleep on shared surfaces without the protection of clean linens. Infants should be placed to sleep on their backs, but allowed to assume their favorite sleeping positions independently thereafter. A physician's note is required for exemption from this practice. Sleeping infants should be in a crib or otherwise protected.

In the example for indicator 1.2, "crowded" means that cribs/cots/mats for children under 2 years of age are placed so they are less than 36 inches away from one another. This distance is required for control of airborne infection in very young children who are less able to fight off disease. For children 2 years and older, "crowded" means cots/mats are less than 18 inches apart. Tighter spacing is permissible if rest equipment is separated by a solid barrier, and provider has easy access to all children.

3.3. "Sufficient supervision" means that provider is present to protect children's health and safety and to supervise children who are awake. Provider is alert and can visually supervise infants; toddlers and preschoolers can be heard, and are visually checked periodically during nap.

5.3. If nap is not observed, judge the quality of the supervision primarily on what was observed throughout the observation as well as information provided on how nap supervision is handled.

Questions

If nap is not observed, ask: Since I was not here to see naptime, how is nap handled? *More specific questions can then be asked:*

1.2. Where do the children sleep? How are the cots/mats arranged?

1.3, 3.3, 5.3. Who supervises naptime? How is supervision handled?

3.1. What do you do if a child is tired before naptime?

7.2. What do you do if a child wakes up very early from nap?

Inadequate		Minimal		Good		Excellent
1	2	3	4	5	6	7

9. Meals/snacks

1.1 Meal/snack schedule is inappropriate (Ex. children made to wait even if hungry or tired).*

1.2 Food served does not meet nutrition guidelines or is not appropriate (Ex. foods that might cause choking; foods/beverages too hot).*

1.3 Basic sanitary procedures usually neglected.*

1.4 Inappropriate feeding practices used (Ex. infants not held for bottle feeding; toddlers unsupervised while eating; children eat or drink when walking, playing, lying down; manners enforced harshly; children forced to eat).*

1.5 No accommodations made for children's food allergies or family dietary restrictions.
NA permitted.

3.1 Meal/snack schedule meets each child's needs (Ex. infants on individual schedules; children given snack if hungry before lunch; snack available for school-agers).*

3.2 Well-balanced age-appropriate food served for meals and snacks.*

3.3 Basic sanitary procedures maintained at least half of the time.*

3.4 Appropriate feeding practices used (adequate supervision for ages and abilities of children).

3.5 Allergies/dietary restrictions posted, and food/beverage substitutions made.
NA permitted.

5.1 Meal/snack times well organized (Ex. food prepared ahead of time; different ages fed to avoid waiting; children safely involved in activities while provider prepares food and/or allowed to help).

5.2 Meals/snacks are relaxed and pleasant (Ex. provider patient with messiness; slow eaters given plenty of time; conversations involving provider and children).

5.3 Basic sanitary procedures usually practiced.*

5.4 Menus provided for parents (Ex. posted in family child care home or copy given to parents).*
NA permitted.

7.1 Provider uses meal/snack times to encourage learning (Ex. names foods for infants and toddlers; provides child-sized eating and serving utensils to encourage self-help skills; school-agers prepare own snack).

7.2 Provider cooperates with parents to establish good eating habits (Ex. plan together to help child give up bottle; coordinate introduction of new foods; decide on nutritional foods for children to bring from home).

(See Notes for Clarification and Questions on next page)

1.1, 1.2, 3.1, 3.2. To determine appropriate schedule and nutritional adequacy, refer to nutrition guidelines for ages of children enrolled in the USDA Child Care and Adult Food Program or comparable guidelines from other countries. Check menu in addition to observing food served. If no menu is available, ask the provider to describe meals/snacks served. If parents provide food, provider must check nutritional adequacy and supplement when needed. An occasional instance of not meeting the guidelines—for example, cupcakes for a birthday party instead of the regular snack—should not affect the rating. Drinking water should be available or offered between meals/snacks to children who eat solid foods.

Foods that are too hot are not considered appropriate, such as food or bottles warmed in a microwave oven or in water warmer than 120 degrees.

1.3, 3.3, 5.3. Basic sanitary procedures:
- Provider washes hands, even if gloves are used, before and after both bottle feeding and preparing and serving food to children, or whenever contaminated during feeding or serving food.
- Children who feed themselves have hands washed before and after eating. Re-contamination of hands after being washed should be minimized by having children begin eating as soon as hands have been washed.
- Eating surfaces (such as highchair trays or table top) cleaned and sanitized before and after serving food.
- No contaminated food should be fed to the child (e.g., perishable food brought from home that is not refrigerated; food that has been touched by another child). Utensils, not hands, should be used to cut up food, serve, or feed a child.

- For milk and juice in bottles to be considered sanitary, they can be unrefrigerated for no longer than 1 hour.
- Any leftover food fed from a container may not be used for a later feeding and must be discarded.
- For information on proper storage and serving, consult *Caring for Our Children: The National Health and Safety Performance Standards for Out-of-Home Child Care, 2nd edition* (American Academy of Pediatrics, 2002).

1.3, 5.3. "Usually " means at least 75% of the time.

1.4. Infants and young toddlers who can sit up independently and hold their bottles may be allowed to feed themselves with close supervision.

5.4. NA if parents provide all food for their children, and no supplementary food is provided. If provider supplements food to meet requirements of 3.2, parents must be notified.

Questions

1.2, 3.2. What do you do if parents provide insufficient food for their children or if the food they provide does not meet children's needs?

1.5, 3.5. What do you do if children have food allergies or families have dietary restrictions?

7.2. Do you have a chance to talk with parents about their child's nutrition? *If yes, ask*: What sort of issues do you discuss?

Inadequate		Minimal		Good		Excellent
1	2	3	4	5	6	7

10. Diapering/toileting

1.1 Sanitary conditions of area are not usually maintained (Ex. potty chairs not sanitized; diapers not disposed of properly; diapering surface not sanitized after each use; toilets not flushed).*

1.2 Major problems with meeting diapering/toileting needs (Ex. diapers rarely changed; children forced to sit on toilet too long; lack of provisions such as paper towels, running water, soap, or sanitizing solution).

1.3 Handwashing often neglected by provider or children after diapering/toileting.*

1.4 Inadequate or unpleasant supervision of children.*

3.1 Sanitary conditions are maintained at least half of the time (Ex. if 1 sink is used, it is sanitized between diapering/toileting and any other use; potty chairs are emptied, cleaned, and sanitized after each use).*

3.2 Diapering/toileting needs usually met in an appropriate manner (Ex. individual schedules that include visual checks of the diaper at least every 2 hours; toileting supplies readily available).*

3.3 Provider and children usually wash hands after diapering/toileting.*

3.4 Adequate supervision for ages and abilities of children.

5.1 Sanitary conditions usually maintained.*

5.2 Sanitary conditions easy to maintain (Ex. no potty chairs used; warm running water near diapering area and toilets; easy-to-clean surfaces).

5.3 Pleasant provider–child interaction.

7.1 Sanitary conditions always maintained.*

7.2 Provisions convenient and accessible (Ex. steps to reach sink and toilet; handrail for child with disability; toileting area adjacent to room; easy-to-reach storage for diapering next to changing table; diaper changing arrangement is comfortable for provider to use).*

7.3 Self-help skills promoted as children are ready.

*Notes for Clarification

1.1, 3.1, 5.1, 7.1. The purpose of maintaining sanitary conditions is to prevent the spread of germs in the urine or stool to the provider or child's hands, the diapering surface, containers of supplies, cabinet doors, or any other surface the children and provider might touch. Wearing of gloves for diaper changing is optional, but helpful. A fresh solution of bleach water should be made up daily, 1 tablespoon of household bleach to 1 quart of water (or ¼ cup bleach to 1 gallon of water), or an EPA-registered sanitizer should be used according to the manufacturer's instructions.

The following measures are essential to cut down on the spread of gastro-intestinal illness and should be considered when scoring this item. The provider should:

I. Prepare for diapering/changing soiled clothing

- To minimize contamination outside of the changing area
  —One diaper-changing area should be selected and used consistently.

  —The diaper changing area should be physically separated from the food preparation and serving areas, including separate sinks. If the same sink must be used for more than diapering/toileting, faucet handles and sink should be sanitized with a bleach and water solution after diapering/toileting use.
  —The diapering surface must be non-porous so it can be sanitized after each diaper change with a bleach/water solution (i.e., no cloth quilted pads or fabric safety straps, no containers stored on the diapering surface).
  —If paper is used to cover the changing surface, it should be long enough to cover from the child's shoulders to heels (in case it becomes soiled and must be folded over to give a clean surface during the change).
- To prepare for a change before bringing the child to area, have ready
  —Enough wipes for the change (including wiping the bottom and hands after removing the soiled diaper/clothing) removed from the box.

1.1, 3.1, 5.1, 7.1. (cont.)

    —A clean diaper or underwear, plastic bag for soiled clothes, and clean clothes if soiled clothing is changed.

    —Non-porous gloves if they will be used, and a dab of diaper cream on a disposable piece of paper or tissue if cream is being used.

II. Follow diapering/changing procedure

- Prepare for changing as indicated above.
- Place child on changing surface. Remove clothing to access diaper or soiled clothing. If soiled, place clothes into plastic bag.
- Remove soiled diaper and place into lined, hands-free trash container. Clothing must be sealed in a plastic bag without being rinsed, and sent home.
- Use wipes to clean child's bottom from front to back.
- Use a wipe to remove soil from adult's hands.
- Use another wipe to remove soil from child's hands.
- Throw soiled wipes into lined, hands-free trash container.
- Put on clean diaper or underwear and redress child.
- Move child to sink and wash hands following the "handwashing procedure."
- Spray diapering surface with a soap-water solution to clean. Wipe dry with disposable towel.
- Spray diapering surface with bleach-water solution and wait at least 2 minutes before wiping with disposable towel or allow to air dry. The surface cannot be sprayed and immediately wiped.
- Wash own hands using the "handwashing procedure," without contaminating any other surface.

III. Take additional precautions for diapering/toileting

- Toilets must be flushed after each use.
- Floors/other surfaces that become contaminated must be sanitized.
- Toys that are played with or objects that are touched during diapering/toileting must be put aside to be sanitized.
- Other surfaces should not be contaminated during changing or toileting unless properly sanitized. For example, if child is changed on a pad on the floor, soiled diaper should not be placed on floor unless floor is sanitized afterwards.
- Note: Provider's hands must be washed after the changing procedure is completed, after diaper checks, and after helping children with toileting. Children's hands must be washed after diapering and toileting.

1.1, 3.1. If the same sink is used by either children or adults for both diapering/toileting and food-related routines (including toothbrushing) or for other purposes (to wash toys/other classroom equipment; after wiping nose), it must be sanitized by spraying sink and faucets with a bleach solution after diapering/toileting use. As an exception to this rule, in order to avoid requiring children to wash hands in quick succession between toileting and being fed, the following applies: if children use toilet, wash hands and then immediately sit down for meal/snack, contamination of children's hands at toileting sink must be minimized by having children/adults turn off faucet with paper towel.

1.3, 3.3. Handwashing for infants, toddlers, older children, and provider requires that hands be washed with liquid soap and warm running water for at least 10 seconds.

- Thorough handwashing of child's hands with liquid soap and warm running water is required after each diapering/toileting is completed. Using wipes or antiseptic waterless washes cannot be substituted for handwashing. To avoid injury of a child in very unusual circumstances (e.g., a new-born baby with no head control, a very heavy baby with little body control), use of a disposable wipe is an acceptable substitute.
- Thorough adult handwashing with warm running water and soap is required after each diaper check, each diaper change, changing soiled clothing, helping child with toileting, and as the final step after the diapering surface has been sanitized. This must be done before any other surfaces in the home are touched. Handwashing after diapering is usually completed after spraying the diapering surface with a sanitizing solution. If the surface is allowed to dry for 2 or more minutes and then wiped dry, a *second* washing of hands is not required.

1.4. "Inadequate supervision" means that the provider does not monitor to protect the safety of the children or to ensure that sanitary procedures (such as handwashing) are carried out.

3.1, 5.1, 7.1. Use the chart on the scoresheet to track maintenance of sanitary conditions of diapering/toileting. Any other major problems related to toileting that results in substantial contamination result in a score of "No" for this indicator. For example, floor contaminated around toilet without being cleaned and sanitized, toilets flushed less than half of the time after use.

3.2, 3.3, 5.1. "Usually" means that procedures are carried out 75% of the time during the observation, and no major problem is observed.

7.2. A diaper changing arrangement that is comfortable for the provider to use prevents back injuries or uncomfortable movements.

Inadequate		Minimal		Good		Excellent
1	2	3	4	5	6	7

11. Health practices*

1.1 Provider does not usually act to cut down on the spread of germs (Ex. handwashing often neglected; toys and furnishings dirty; pets not immunized; signs of animal contamination in space used by children; floors and rugs not clean; noses rarely wiped).

1.2 Smoking/drinking alcohol/using illegal drugs occurs in child care areas, either indoors or outdoors. (Ex. cigarette waste left in play area; provider smokes while supervising children outdoors).

1.3 Children with contagious illness are not removed from contact with others (Ex. children with diarrhea not excluded from group).*

3.1 Provider acts to cut down on the spread of germs at least half of the time (Ex. mouthed toys washed daily; different towel/washcloth used for each child; toothbrushes stored to avoid contamination; tissues used when needed and disposed of properly; pets handled to minimize health risks; no shared use of personal items such as combs, brushes).

3.2 Hands of children and provider washed at least 75% of the time when needed to protect health.*

3.3 Extra clothes available and children changed when needed.

3.4 All medications administered properly.*
NA permitted.

5.1 Provider usually acts to cut down on the spread of germs (Ex. litter boxes, pet food, and toys kept out of children's reach; sandbox used by children covered when not in use).*

5.2 Hands of children and the provider consistently washed to protect health, with only 1 or 2 lapses.

5.3 Children are properly cared for to meet health needs indoors and outdoors (Ex. dressed properly; wet or soiled clothes changed; sun protection when outdoors).*

5.4 Provider is a good model of health practices (Ex. eats only healthful foods in front of children; dresses properly for weather; fingernails easily cleaned).

7.1 Children encouraged to manage health practices independently (Ex. provider talks to infants about health practices as they are being done; proper handwashing technique taught; health-related books, pictures, songs used; school-agers reminded to wash hands and brush teeth).

7.2 Individual toothbrushes used at least once daily in full-day program.*
NA permitted.

7.3 Provider has arranged for a health consultant (Ex. local doctor, nurse, child care health consultant) to handle child care related questions.

(See Notes for Clarification and Questions on next page)

Notes for Clarification

Item 11. Health practices associated with nap/rest (item 8), meals/snacks (item 9), and diapering/toileting (item 10) are covered in those items. Therefore, these practices should not be considered in scoring this item.

1.3. Valid reasons for exclusion include: (1) fever with a behavior change that indicates that a child is unable to participate in the program; (2) a child requires more care than the caregiver can reasonably provide and still care for the other children; (3) a child has a condition, such as diarrhea, that requires exclusion to protect the other children from being exposed to a transmissible infectious disease. Common colds are most transmissible before symptoms appear and during the early watery discharge phase of the illness. Green and yellow nasal mucus are not signs of transmissible infectious disease.

3.2. See definition of handwashing on page 10. This percentage should be calculated separately for the provider and for children. In this item, examples of when handwashing is necessary for provider and children include:

- Upon arrival at the home, when reentering the home after outdoor play
- Before shared water play and after messy, sand, or water play
- After dealing with bodily fluids (Ex. running noses, vomit, blood) or making significant skin contact when open sores exist
- After touching contaminated objects (trashcan lids, the floor) or pets.

3.4. Only medications that have been prescribed by a physician for a particular child are to be given ~~...~~ ations only from original ~~...~~ Older school-agers may ~~...~~ re NA if no children are in

5.1. "Usually" means that there are no major problems with sanitary procedures, only an occasional lapse, such as failing to quickly wipe a child's nose or disposing of a used tissue improperly.

5.3. Children should be dressed so they are neither hot nor cold (e.g., sweatshirts not worn outdoors in hot weather, wet clothes changed on chilly day); children have shade in the play area and/or use sun protection such as sun screen, hats, and sun-protective clothing when they are outside between 10 AM and 2 PM on overcast or sunny days.

7.2. Score NA for programs open 6 hours or less per day or if only infants are enrolled. If toothpaste is used, a pea-sized amount is put on each child's brush from some that has been squeezed from the tube onto disposable paper for each child, so that no child's paste is contaminated with another child's brush. Water should be provided for rinsing.

Questions

1.2. Is smoking allowed in the child care areas, either indoors or outdoors?

3.3. Are extra clothes available for the children, in case they are needed?

7.3. Is there a health professional you can ask when you have health questions related to child care?

Inadequate		Minimal		Good		Excellent
1	2	3	4	5	6	7

12. Safety practices

1.1 Four or more hazards that could result in serious injury indoors.*

1.2 Four or more hazards that could result in serious injury outdoors.*

1.3 Inadequate supervision to protect children's safety indoors and outdoors (Ex. provider occupied with other tasks; no supervision near areas of potential danger; infants, toddlers, and preschoolers not within sight except for momentary lapses).

3.1 No more than 3 safety hazards that could result in serious injury indoors and outdoors, combined.*

3.2 Adequate supervision to protect children's safety indoors and outdoors.

3.3 Essentials needed to handle emergencies available (Ex. well stocked first aid kit; written emergency procedures posted; adult present who is trained in pediatric first aid and CPR; working smoke alarm and fire extinguisher; substitute provider available for emergencies).

5.1 No safety hazards that could cause serious injury indoors or outdoors.

5.2 Provider usually anticipates and takes action to eliminate safety hazards (Ex. removes toys under climbing equipment; closes gate or locks dangerous areas to keep children in safe space; wipes up spills to prevent falls).

5.3 Home has passed official fire inspection, and emergency evacuation procedures are practiced monthly with children.

7.1 Provider ensures that children follow safety rules (Ex. prevents crowding on slides; no climbing on furniture; requires school-agers to use helmets and other safety equipment when needed).

7.2 Provider explains reasons for safety rules to children (Ex. "We are nice to our friends, biting hurts"; "Be careful, it's hot").

---

*Notes for Clarification

1.1, 1.2, 3.1. Be sure to note all safety problems on score sheet. When determining how serious a hazard is, consider location, characteristics of children, and relative likelihood of a problem. The following lists of hazards are not meant to be complete.

Some *indoor* safety hazards:
- No safety protection on electrical outlets; electrical cords accessible to very young children
- Strings, cords that might cause strangulation accessible to children
- Heavy objects or furniture child can pull down
- Medicines, cleaning materials, pesticides, aerosols, and substances labeled "keep out of reach of children" not locked away
- Bleach solution used when children can inhale the spray (e.g., while children are sitting at table)
- Walkers that a child can move across the floor or beanbag chairs used for infants
- Water, or any surface accessible to children, too hot (e.g., is too hot for an adult to touch for at least 30 seconds or measures more than 120 degrees F using a meat thermometer)

- Thumbtacks or staples used where very young children can reach Crib/playpen slats or mesh sides permit entrapment (e.g., slats more than 2⅜ inches apart; crib sides not locked; a mesh playpen with collapsible sides)
- Tripping hazards such as mats or rugs that have foot-catching edges or that slide
- Unprotected radiator, heater, or fireplace in use
- Open stairwells accessible (including those that have climbable railings or places a child could slip through)
- Small objects that can cause choking accessible to infants/toddlers (e.g., objects less than 1¼ inch diameter and 2½ inches long, or spheres less than 1¾ inches in diameter)
- No 6-inch raised edge as protection from falling off diapering table
- Crib mattress that does not fit snugly (e.g., allows 2 or more fingers to be inserted between it and the crib side)
- Toys hung across crib of a child who can sit up or get to hands and knees and hang him/herself

1.1, 1.2, 3.1. (cont.)

- Babies put to sleep on stomach or side instead of on their backs
- Provider picks up infants/toddlers by arm or hand, putting child at risk for joint injury
- Cribs that are difficult for adults to raise and lower the side and do not provide at least 20 inches from the top of the mattress to the top of the crib rail
- Styrofoam objects, plastic bags, or latex (rubber) balloons accessible to children
- Possibility of unsupervised access for infants/toddlers to any container of water (e.g., toilets, 5-gallon buckets)
- Guns or ammunition present in space used for child care; or any guns in home not locked away unloaded, with firing pin removed. Ammunition not locked away, separated from gun.
- Since *older infants* will pull themselves up on anything within reach, all furnishings accessible to them should withstand this without toppling, shaking, or collapsing. If swings and rocking chairs are part of the furnishings accessible to infants, they should be placed so that children are less likely to pull up on them than on more stable furniture. If they are placed so that children frequently use them to pull up, they should be counted as a safety hazard.
- Home has not passed an official fire inspection.

Some *outdoor* safety hazards:

- Play area not contained by fence or barrier that prevents children from leaving designated safe area
- Unfenced swimming pool; pool accessible without adequate supervision
- Tools not meant for children's use are accessible
- All dangerous substances (e.g., labeled "keep out of reach of children") not locked away
- Sharp or dangerous objects present

- Unsafe walkway or stairs accessible to children
- Children can gain independent access to road or driveways
- Hazardous trash accessible
- Play equipment too high (e.g., more than 1 foot per year of age above fall surface), not well maintained, not stable. Play equipment that poses threat of head entrapment with openings that are between 3½ inches and 9 inches across, or finger entrapment with openings between ⅜ inch and 1 inch. Other dangers include injury from pinch-points, projections, or insufficient cushioned fall zones.
- Children transported in provider's vehicle without appropriate safety precautions (e.g., proper restraints not used, children left in car unsupervised)
- Trampolines used

Questions

1.2, 3.1, 5.1, 5.2. Do you ever transport children? How is this handled to ensure their safety?

3.3. What provisions do you have for handling emergencies?

5.3. Has your home passed an official fire inspection? Do you practice emergency evacuation procedures such as fire drills? How often?

Specific follow-up questions may be needed, such as:

How would you handle an emergency?

Do you (or anyone else who works in the home) have training in first aid appropriate for all age groups enrolled, including management of a blocked airway (choke-saving) and rescue breathing?

Is there a first aid kit available for you to use? Can you please show it to me?

Is there a telephone accessible you would use to call for help in an emergency?

Inadequate		Minimal		Good		Excellent
1	2	3	4	5	6	7

LISTENING AND TALKING

13. Helping children understand language*

1.1 Little or no talking to children.

1.2 Loud noise often interferes with children's ability to hear language (Ex. loud music or television on most of day; much crying throughout the day).

1.3 Provider often talks to children in an unpleasant manner (Ex. harsh tone of voice; frequent threats; discouraging or negative statements).

1.4 Provider uses a very limited vocabulary when talking to children (Ex. uses "it, this, that" instead of names of objects or actions; uses few descriptive words; talks about a limited range of topics).

3.1 Moderate amount of talking to children during routines or play.

3.2 Reasonably quiet in the home so children can hear language.

3.3 Provider usually talks to children in a neutral or pleasant tone of voice.

3.4 Content of talk is generally encouraging and positive rather than discouraging and negative.

5.1 Provider talks to the children frequently throughout the day during both routines and play.*

5.2 Provider talk is meaningful to children (Ex. talks about things children are experiencing).

5.3 Verbal communication is personalized (Ex. makes eye contact with child; uses child's name; talks to child in child's primary language; uses signing or alternative communication when needed).

5.4 Provider usually uses descriptive words for objects and actions in communication with children.*

7.1 Provider uses a wide range of exact words in communicating with children (Ex. names many different objects and actions; uses descriptive words).*

7.2 Provider talks about many different topics with the children (Ex. talks about feelings; expresses child's intentions with words in addition to naming objects and actions).

7.3 Provider adjusts complexity of language to match children's abilities (Ex. uses more complex sentences with older children; uses simpler sentences with children whose primary language differs from the provider's).

*Notes for Clarification

Item 13. While indicators for quality in this item hold true across a diversity of cultures and individuals, the ways in which they are expressed may differ. For example, tone of voice may differ, with some individuals using excited voices while others may be quieter. Whatever the personal communication styles of the provider being observed, the requirements of the indicators must be met, although there can be some variation in the way that this is done.

Because the frequency and content of language interactions are very important in influencing the development of children's language abilities, score indicators based on what is observed as a regular practice throughout the observation. Examples of meeting the requirements should occur throughout the observation, not just as a single instance.

5.1. Although the provider may talk more to one child than another, to give credit there can be no obvious ignoring of any child.

5.4. In determining whether the language is descriptive, ask yourself if you could tell what the provider is talking about to children just by listening and not looking. Exact, descriptive words are used in "James, bring the red truck to me" rather than "Bring that to me."

7.1. While indicator 5.4 requires that the provider "usually uses descriptive words," the number of words may be limited. Indicator 7.1 requires the use of many different words, characteristic of a "wide vocabulary."

Inadequate		Minimal		Good		Excellent
1	2	3	4	5	6	7

14. Helping children use language

1.1 Children's verbal or nonverbal communication is discouraged much of the day (Ex. provider responds negatively; children often told to be quiet; babies ignored or kept isolated).

1.2 Talking used only to control children's behavior (Ex. provider does not have conversations with children or encourage them to communicate).

3.1 Moderate amount of verbal or non-verbal positive response to children's communication throughout the day; little or no ignoring of children or negative response.*

3.2 Some encouragement of children's communication (Ex. attempts to interpret what child is trying to say; listens attentively; asks questions).*

3.3 Some social talking with children throughout the day (Ex. conversations about child's interests; verbal play with babies; school-agers asked about their day).

3.4 Children allowed to talk much of the day.

5.1 Provider generally responds in a timely and positive manner to children's attempts to communicate and follows through appropriately (Ex. crying answered quickly; attends to verbal requests; responds to children's communications during play).

5.2 Provider frequently encourages children to communicate with her throughout the day.

5.3 Provider encourages children to communicate with one another (Ex. school-agers work on project together; toddlers shown how to use words to avoid conflicts; children taught sign language to use with others).*
NA permitted.

5.4 Provider has many turn-taking conversations with children (Ex. imitates infant sounds in a back-and-forth "baby conversation"; repeats what toddler says, and then lets toddler add more; discusses ideas with older children).*

7.1 Provider adds more words and ideas to what children say (Ex. when toddler says "juice" provider responds with "Here is your orange juice. It's in your cup.").*
NA permitted.

7.2 Provider asks children questions to encourage more complex answers (Ex. asks and answers questions for infants; young children asked "what" or "where" questions; older children asked "why" or "how" questions).

7.3 Provider usually maintains a good balance between listening and talking (Ex. gives child time to process information and answer; more talking for infants; even turns with older children).

7.4 Provider links older children's talk with writing (Ex. writes what children dictate and reads it back; school-agers write stories, use email).*
NA permitted.

*Notes for Clarification

3.1. "Moderate amount" requires a positive response by the provider at least half of the time children attempt to communicate, no negative responses to children, and little or no ignoring of children's attempts to communicate.

3.2. At least half the time throughout the observation, the provider must be observed attempting to correctly interpret what children try to communicate.

5.3. Score NA if only one child is present during the observation. To give credit, 2 examples must be observed. Provider can "encourage" communication among children by modeling conversation, by setting up activities that require communication such as games for 2 children, by having a relaxed social atmosphere, and by helping children communicate their thoughts and intentions to one another.

5.4. Although turn taking in conversations (listening and responding) is always required, the roles of provider and child change as the child becomes more competent in communication. For example, a conversation with a baby or toddler is usually shorter and requires more input from the provider. As children become more verbal, the balance between listening and talking should become more equal, because the provider is encouraging children to use language.

7.1. Score NA when all children present during the observation are non-verbal.

7.4. NA is permitted if only infants and toddlers are enrolled. A score of "Yes" can be given if there is evidence in observed interaction or display of linking written with spoken language, while preschool and school-age children are present in the family child care home. Credit is not given if only the child's name or date of work is recorded.

Inadequate		Minimal		Good		Excellent
1	2	3	4	5	6	7

15. Using books

1.1 If one age group is enrolled, fewer than 6 appropriate books are accessible daily. If more than one age group is enrolled, fewer than 3 appropriate books are accessible for each age group.*

1.2 Books generally in poor repair (Ex. torn or incomplete books; tattered pictures; books scribbled on).

1.3 Books not read to children daily (Ex. provider or older school-agers do not read to younger children).*
NA permitted.

3.1 At least 6 appropriate books but no less than 3 for each age group enrolled accessible daily, for much of the day.*

3.2 Almost all books are in good repair.*

3.3 Provider reads books with children daily (either provider- or child-initiated).*
NA permitted.

3.4 Participation encouraged only while children are interested; children not forced to participate.

5.1 At least 12 appropriate books for each age group, but no less than 2 for each child in each age group accessible daily for much of the day.*

5.2 A wide selection of books is accessible.*

5.3 Provider reads books informally with individuals or very small groups of interested children daily.*
NA permitted.

5.4 Book times are pleasant and interactive (Ex. infant enjoys being held while book is read; toddler shows interest in turning pages and pointing to pictures; preschoolers allowed to ask questions and make comments; older children discuss content).*

7.1 Books gathered together in one or more locations for convenient and comfortable use by children (Ex. basket of books for infants/toddlers on rug away from active play; books for older children out of young children's reach near soft furnishings).

7.2 Provider is involved in using books with children periodically throughout the day.*

7.3 Provider encourages children in all age groups enrolled to read at their ability level (Ex. names pictures for infants; helps toddlers identify pictures and turn pages; shows preschoolers how words match pictures; listens and helps while school-agers read; encourages fluent reader to read to younger children).*

7.4 Books are added or changed to maintain interest.

(See Notes for Clarification and Questions on next page)

*Notes for Clarification

1.1, 3.1, 5.1. Age groups include infant/toddler, preschool/kindergarten, and school-age. Examples of appropriate children's books: infant/toddler—sturdy vinyl, cloth, or hard-page picture books; preschool/kindergarten—books with easy to understand content and attractive pictures; school-age—longer books, some with chapters, content and difficulty matches abilities of children enrolled. Books may be home-made or commercially produced.

1.3, 3.3, 5.3. Score NA if all children enrolled are fluent readers.

3.1. Count only complete books with covers and all pages to give credit for the indicator. Books that are not appropriate for the children in the age group (e.g., too difficult, too easy, frightening, violent) cannot be counted as any of the required books.

3.2. "Good repair" means that the book has an intact cover, and the pages are not torn, scribbled on, or missing. Minor problems (small tears, slight scribble, chew marks) that do not interfere with the use of the books are acceptable. "Almost all" means no more than 3 books may be in poor repair.

5.1. To give credit, none of the books accessible to kindergarten age or younger may be violent or frightening.

5.2. A wide selection includes books about people of varying races, ages, and abilities; animals; familiar experiences and includes both fiction and factual information. A wide selection is required for each age group. Some books may be suitable for more than one age group.

5.3. At least 1 instance must be observed to give credit for this indicator.

5.4. This indicator refers to book times with the provider and any child, and must be observed to give credit.

7.2. At least 2 instances must be observed to give credit. For example, reading to a small group or an individual, pointing out pictures in book for baby, using book to help school-ager with homework.

7.3. Must be observed with at least one age group to give credit.

Questions

7.4. Do you add to or change the books that are put out for the children to use? *If yes, ask:* How often do you do this? What kinds of books are added?

Inadequate		Minimal		Good		Excellent
1	2	3	4	5	6	7

ACTIVITIES

16. Fine motor

1.1 No appropriate fine motor materials for each age group enrolled, accessible for daily use.*

1.2 Materials are generally in poor repair.

3.1 Some appropriate fine motor materials for each age group, accessible for daily use.*

3.2 Materials required in 3.1 are accessible for much of the day.

3.3 Materials generally in good repair.

5.1 Many and varied appropriate fine motor materials for each age group, accessible for much of the day.*

5.2 Materials are well-organized for independent use (Ex. similar toys stored together; sets of toys in separate containers; toys picked up, sorted, and restored as needed).

5.3 Provider interacts with children in relation to their play with the materials (Ex. talks to baby about sound of shaken rattle; helps child to fit puzzle pieces; shows older child how to use thimble).*

7.1 Additional fine motor materials rotated monthly to provide variety.

7.2 Space used for play with fine motor materials is convenient (Ex. school-age materials out of reach of younger children; several materials can be used at same time without confusion; materials placed within reach of non-mobile children).

(See Notes for Clarification and Questions on next page)

1.1, 3.1, 5.1. Appropriate fine motor materials are safe, challenging but not frustrating, and may include household items. Examples are:

- **Infant**: rattles, grasping toys, busy boxes, nested cups, containers to fill and dump, textured toys, cradle gyms, household items such as graduated measuring cups, pots with lids.
- **Toddler**: shape sorting games, large stringing beads, big pegs with peg boards, simple puzzles, pop beads, stacking rings, nesting toys, medium or large interlocking blocks, crayons.
- **Preschool–K**: *interlocking building toys* with pieces of any size; *manipulatives* such as stringing beads, lacing cards, pegs with peg boards, links and gears, small table blocks; *art materials* such as crayons and scissors; and *puzzles*.
- **School-Age**: appropriately challenging materials in the types listed above for Preschool–K: *building toys* such as Lincoln Logs, small interlocking block building sets; *manipulatives* such as pick-up sticks, jacks, marbles, small computer games, *art and craft materials* such as markers, watercolors, jewelry making, weaving, sewing; and *puzzles* which are more complex (with many and/or small pieces).

3.1. "Some" for infants and toddlers requires at least 5 different appropriate materials. For preschool and school-age children, "some" means at least 2 different materials from each of the 4 types of materials for each age group enrolled.

5.1. "Many and varied" for infants and toddlers means at least 10 different appropriate materials. For preschool and school-age children, "many and varied" means at least 3 different appropriate materials from each of the 4 types. Some materials may be appropriate for more than one age group.

5.3. To give credit at least two instances must be observed.

Questions

7.1. Do you have any additional fine motor materials that you use with the children? *If yes, ask:* Could you please show these to me?

Inadequate		Minimal		Good		Excellent
1	2	3	4	5	6	7

17. Art*

1.1 No appropriate art materials provided for use by children.*

1.2 Toxic or unsafe materials are used for art (Ex. shaving cream, glitter, permanent markers, acrylic or oil paints, things young children can choke on such as styrofoam peanuts or small beads).*

3.1 At least one appropriate drawing material used with toddlers (12–30 months) at least once a week; at least one drawing material accessible daily for preschoolers and older children.*

3.2 All art materials used with children are nontoxic, and safe.*

3.3 Children not required to participate; alternative activities available.

3.4 Some individual expression permitted with art materials (Ex. children allowed to decorate pre-cut shapes in their own way; in addition to provider-directed projects, some individualized work is permitted).*

5.1 Toddlers offered some appropriate art material 3 times a week; preschoolers and older children have drawing materials accessible daily for much of the day.*

5.2 At least two different materials from 4 of the types of art materials are accessible daily to preschoolers and older children.* *NA permitted.*

5.3 Individual expression encouraged (Ex. expectations based on children's abilities; children carry out work in their own way).*

5.4 Provider facilitates appropriate use of materials (Ex. tapes paper in place for scribbling; uses adaptive equipment when needed; encourages children to paint on paper and not on furniture or walls).

7.1 At least 3 different drawing materials are used with toddlers weekly (Ex. crayons, washable watercolor markers, and chalk); at least 3 different materials from 4 of the types accessible daily for preschoolers and older children.

7.2 Access to materials is based on children's abilities (Ex. made accessible only with close supervision for toddlers and twos; accessible for independent use by preschoolers and older children).

7.3 Three-dimensional art materials used at least monthly with preschoolers and older children. *NA permitted.*

(See Notes for Clarification and Questions on next page)

Item 17. Mark this item NA if all children in group are younger than 12 months of age. However, if art activities are used with infants, the possible health, safety, and supervision problems should be considered in the appropriate items.

1.1, 3.1, 5.1, 5.2. Types of art materials include: *drawing materials* such as paper with crayons, nontoxic markers, pencils; *paints*; *three-dimensional materials* such as play dough, clay, wood gluing, or carpentry; *collage materials*; *tools* such as safe scissors, staplers, hole punches, tape dispensers. Only the simplest materials should be used with toddlers and twos. Other materials should be added as children gain skills and ability to use materials appropriately. Coloring books and photocopied pages are not given credit for art, but are considered in Item 16. Fine motor. Edible materials (such as chocolate pudding, dried pasta, popcorn, and so forth) cannot be counted as art materials because they give a misleading message about the proper use of food. The possible health (sanitary issues), safety (e.g., choking hazards), and supervision consequences of using food in art should be considered in Items 11, 12, and/or 27.

1.1. If any appropriate art materials are provided for use by any child (for an hour daily), in any age group, score 1.1 "No."

1.2, 3.2. All art materials must be non-toxic and safe.

3.1. In groups with children under 3 years of age or with some developmental delays, the provider may bring out materials to make them accessible daily with close supervision for as long as there is interest. Some adaptations may be needed to make art materials accessible and usable for children with disabilities. To give credit, the materials must be accessible daily for at least 1 hour in an 8 hour program, prorated appropriately for shorter programs (see chart in "Explanation of Terms Used Throughout the Scale" on page 9).

3.4. "Individual expression" means that each child may select the subject matter and/or art medium, and carry out the work in his or her own way. A number of paintings, each of which is different because the children have not been asked to copy a model, is considered "individual expression."

5.3. *Individual expression encouraged* means that 85% of the time when art materials are used, children can do "free art" and are not required to follow an example. Observe to see whether children have access to the art materials and if they actually use them in their own creative way. You may also look at the artwork displayed in the home. If you see many provider-directed projects displayed, and little individual work being done by the children during the observation, do not give credit for this indicator. If you are not sure, ask the provider how often projects are done that require following an example. If such projects are used no more than once or twice a week, and you observe many instances of children using art materials in their own creative way, you may give credit for 5.3.

Questions

1.1, 1.2, 3.1, 3.2. Are art materials used with the children? *If yes, ask:* What materials are used? May I see these art supplies? Are edible materials ever used for art?

3.1, 5.1, 7.1. How often are art materials used with the children?

7.2. How do you choose what art materials to make accessible to the children?

7.3. Are three-dimensional art materials such as play dough, clay, or wood for gluing ever used? If so, how often?

Inadequate		Minimal		Good		Excellent
1	2	3	4	5	6	7

18. Music and movement

1.1 No music/movement experiences for children.*

1.2 Loud music is on much of the day and interferes with ongoing activities (Ex. constant background music makes conversation in normal tones difficult).

1.3 Children exposed to music with content that is inappropriate (Ex. violent, sexually explicit, presents negative stereotype of any group).

3.1 Some appropriate music materials, toys, or instruments accessible for free play daily (Ex. rattles and other musical toys, simple instruments, CD player or computer with recorded music).*

3.2 Provider initiates at least 1 music or movement activity daily (Ex. sings songs with children; soft music turned on at naptime; plays music for dancing).

3.3 Children not required to participate in group music activities; alternative activities available.

5.1 Many music materials accessible for children's use daily.*

5.2 Some appropriate music materials accessible to each age group for much of the day.*

5.3 Provider informally sings/chants daily with infants, toddlers, preschoolers.*
NA permitted.

5.4 Recorded music is used at limited times and with a positive purpose (Ex. quiet music at nap; put on for dancing or singing and turned off when children lose interest).

7.1 Various types of music are used with children (Ex. classical and popular; music characteristic of different cultures; songs sung in different languages).

7.2 Provider encourages children to dance, clap, or sing along (Ex. dances to music while holding baby; claps to rhythm with toddlers; participates in dance with older children).

7.3 Creativity is encouraged with music activities (Ex. children asked to make up new words to songs, individual dance encouraged).

*Notes for Clarification

1.1. If any child of any age experiences music/movement, score 1.1 "No."

3.1, 5.1. "Music materials" are anything that children can use to create or listen to rhythm, tones, or other types of music, including instruments, noise-making toys, or players for recorded music. Some instruments may be suitable for several age groups. Materials may be homemade or commercially produced. Music heard on TV, video, radio, or computer may be counted. Do not give credit for very short musical sound patterns that are part of computer software. For a tape/CD player to be considered accessible to children 4 years and older, children should be able to use tapes/CDs independently, but younger children may require help from provider.

3.1, 5.2. "Some" means at least 2 materials for use with each age group enrolled.

5.1. "Many" means at least 10 music materials with no fewer than 3 for each age group enrolled.

5.3. To give credit, this indicator must be observed at least once during the observation.

Questions

1.1, 3.2, 5.4. Do you use any music with the children? *If yes, ask:* How is this handled? How often is this done?

3.1, 5.1. Do you have any other musical toys or instruments that the children can use? Could you please show me? When are they used?

7.1. What types of music are used with the children? Can you give me some examples?

Inadequate		Minimal		Good		Excellent
1	2	3	4	5	6	7

19. Blocks*

1.1 No blocks accessible for daily use.*

3.1 Some appropriate blocks for each age group (between 12 months and 7 years), accessible for daily use.*

3.2 Some accessories for blocks accessible daily.*

3.3 Some clear space used for block play.*

5.1 Many blocks and accessories for each age group (between 12 months and 7 years) accessible daily for much of the day.*

5.2 Most blocks and accessories gathered together and sorted by type.*

5.3 Enough space provided for block play, out of traffic, with a steady surface.*

7.1 Sets of 2 different types of blocks for each age group (between 12 months and 7 years) accessible daily for much of the day.*

7.2 Variety of accessories, including transportation toys, people, animals.

7.3 Provider encourages and/or participates in block play with children.*

Notes for Clarification

Item 19. Mark this item NA if all children in care are younger than 12 months or older than 7 years of age.

1.1, 3.1, 5.1, 7.1. Examples of appropriate blocks of various sizes, shapes, colors: **Toddlers:** soft vinyl or cloth covered blocks, large cardboard blocks, sensory blocks such as those that make noises, and any lightweight blocks from the preschool/kindergarten list (such as small wooden unit blocks). **Preschool/kindergarten:** *unit blocks* (wooden, plastic, or hard foam including shapes such as rectangles, squares, triangles, and cylinders); *large hollow blocks* (wooden, plastic, or cardboard); *homemade blocks* (materials such as food boxes and plastic containers). Sensory blocks are not considered appropriate for preschool/kindergarten block play. Note that interlocking blocks (whether large or small) and very small blocks are considered under Item 16. Fine motor, and are not counted here.

1.1. If any blocks are accessible for an hour daily, for any child in any age group enrolled, score 1.1 "No."

3.1. "Some" for toddlers means at least 1 set of 6 blocks of the same type that are stored together; for preschool/early school-age, at least 15 blocks of a specific type that are stored together and can be used by one child to build a modest structure.

3.2, 5.2. Accessories include appropriately-sized toys that can be used with blocks to extend block play, such as small vehicles, people, and animals. Containers to fill and dump may be given credit as accessories for toddlers. Accessories must be placed near the blocks so that children know they are meant to be used with the blocks.

3.3. Any clear space on the floor, a table, etc. meets this requirement.

5.1. "Many" means enough blocks and accessories for each age group to use the materials without undue competition. The actual number needed depends on the age, ability, and number of children enrolled. Toddlers and young twos tend to need fewer blocks than preschool/early school-age children, who can build complex, sizeable structures.

5.2. Perfection is not expected in the sorting of materials. Give credit if materials are clearly organized. Accessories are not mixed up with blocks.

5.3. "Enough space" means that appropriate and satisfying building can take place without interfering with other surrounding activities and without competition for space from children engaged in other play.

7.3. To give credit, this indicator must be observed at least once during the observation.

20. Dramatic play*

1.1 No materials accessible for dramatic play.*

3.1 Some materials accessible daily to carry out meaningful dramatic play (Ex. toy buildings with appropriately sized props; materials to use with dolls; child-sized stove with pots and pans).*

3.2 Some appropriate materials accessible for each age group.*

5.1 Many and varied appropriate dramatic play materials accessible for each age group.*

5.2 Materials for each age group are accessible for much of the day.*

5.3 Materials are organized by type for independent use (Ex. play dishes in separate container; dolls stored together; dress-up hats and purses hung on pegs; accessories stored with toy buildings).

5.4 Some child-sized play furniture for toddlers and preschoolers (Ex. small sink or stove, baby stroller, shopping cart).*
NA permitted.

7.1 Materials provided to represent diversity (Ex. dolls representing different races/cultures; equipment used by people of different cultures or with disabilities).*

7.2 Materials provided for toddlers and older children for active dramatic play outdoors or in other large area.*
NA permitted.

7.3 Provider facilitates children's dramatic play (Ex. talks to toddler on toy telephone; brings out props for playing store; helps school-agers put on a play).*

(See Notes for Clarification on next page)

Item 20. Dramatic play is pretending or making believe. This type of play occurs when children act out roles themselves and when they manipulate figures such as small toy people in a dollhouse or small figures with interlocking blocks. Thus, activities used to teach children to follow specific sequences to properly complete household chores, such as table washing or silver polishing activities, are not counted to meet the requirements of this item. Children must be free to use the materials in their own way, as part of their own make-believe play, to get credit for this item. Dramatic play for infants and toddlers requires very simple props representing familiar experiences. Preschoolers, kindergartners, and school-agers require a wider range of props that they can use to act out their more complex understanding of the world. School-agers often extend their dramatic play into theatrical performances.

Dramatic play is enhanced by props that encourage a variety of themes including *housekeeping* (Ex. dolls, child-sized furniture, dress-up, kitchen utensils); *different kinds of work* (Ex. office, construction, farm, store, fire fighting, transportation); *fantasy* (Ex. animals, dinosaurs, storybook characters); and *leisure* (Ex. camping, sports).

1.1. If any dramatic play materials are accessible to any age group for an hour daily, score 1.1 "No."

3.1. This indicator does not require materials for all age groups.

3.2., 5.1. Materials listed below for one age group may or may not be appropriate for other age groups. For example, baby dolls are appropriate for children in all of the age groups. However, action figures which often display aggression are only appropriate for older school-agers who are able to distinguish between fantasy and reality (3rd to 6th graders).

- **Infants:** dolls, soft animals, pots and pans, toy telephones
- **Toddlers:** dress-up clothes, child-sized house furniture, cooking/eating props, baby dolls and doll furnishings, soft animals, small play buildings with accessories, toy telephones
- **Preschoolers/kindergartners:** in addition to materials listed above for younger children, dress-up clothes representing traditional male and female roles and props to act out work, leisure, or fantasy themes
- **School-agers:** preschool/kindergarten materials plus interlocking blocks with figures and other accessories for fantasy constructions (e.g., pirate ship, castle); dolls representing adult figures; action figures; props for theater play

5.1. Many materials means that children can play without undue competition and that materials are plentiful enough to encourage complex play for older children. For preschoolers and older children, materials for at least 2 themes are required. Variety of materials means that there are many choices for carrying out dramatic play.

5.2. "Materials" refers to the "many and varied" materials required in 5.1.

5.4. Score NA if only infants or school-aged children are enrolled.

7.1. At least two examples are required to give credit.

7.2. Materials provided must be complete enough to permit meaningful pretend play (i.e., stroller has a doll; play house has table, chairs, dishes).

7.3. To give credit, this indicator must be observed at least once

Inadequate		Minimal		Good		Excellent
1	2	3	4	5	6	7

21. Math/number*

1.1 No math/number materials accessible.*

1.2 Math/number taught primarily through rote counting or worksheets.*

1.3 Provider does not talk with children about number or math concepts, such as size and shape, during free play or routines.

3.1 Some developmentally appropriate math/number materials accessible daily for each age group.*

3.2 Provider sometimes talks about math/number concepts during free play or routines.*

5.1 Many and varied appropriate materials accessible.*

5.2 Materials are accessible daily for much of the day.*

5.3 Materials are well organized and in good condition (Ex. sorted by type; all pieces needed for games stored together).*

5.4 Provider talks about math/number concepts during both free play and routines.*

7.1 Materials for all age groups are rotated at least monthly (Ex. teddy bear counters replaced by dinosaur counters; different objects to weigh; math games changed).

7.2 Math/number activities requiring more input from provider are offered for preschoolers and school-agers who attend full day at least every 2 weeks (Ex. making a chart to compare children's height; counting and recording number of birds at bird feeder; cooking projects).*
NA permitted.

7.3 Provider talks about number or math concepts frequently throughout the day with all age groups.

(See Notes for Clarification and Questions on next page)

Notes for Clarification

Item 21. Examples of math/number materials are small objects used in counting activities, balance scales, rulers, number puzzles, magnetic numbers, number games such as dominoes or number lotto, and geometric shapes such as parquetry blocks, books on counting or shapes, math/number computer software.

1.1, 3.1, 5.1. Appropriate math/number materials allow children to use concrete objects to experiment with quantity, size, and shape as they develop the concepts they need for the more abstract tasks required in later school, such as adding, subtracting, and completing paper and pencil math problems. Whether a material or activity is appropriate is based on the abilities and interests of the children. Examples of appropriate materials include:

- **Infants and toddlers**: rattles of various shapes, cradle gyms with hanging shapes, numbers and shape board books, simple shape puzzles, shape sorters, toy telephones and cash registers with numbers, nested cups, stacking rings
- **Preschoolers**: small objects used in counting activities, balance scales, rulers, number puzzles, magnetic numbers, number games such as dominoes or number lotto, and geometric shapes such as parquetry blocks, books on counting or shapes, math/number computer software
- **School-agers**: rulers, tape measures, number lines, unit rods and cubes, parquetry blocks, geo boards, math card and board games, calculators, math computer software

1.1. If any math/number materials are accessible for an hour daily, for any child in any age group enrolled, score 1.1 "No."

1.2. "Primarily taught through rote counting or worksheets" means that such experiences make up the vast majority of children's math/number learning opportunities. Even if rote counting or worksheet use is observed, when scoring this indicator, be sure to consider all math/number experiences throughout the observation.

3.1. "Some" means at least 2 different materials related to number and 2 related to shape. One material may be appropriate for more than one age group. Look around the areas used for child care carefully to find math materials because they might not be gathered together. To give credit, materials must be accessible for 1 hour in programs of 8 hours or more, prorated for programs operating fewer hours. See "Explanation of Terms Used Throughout the Scale" on page 9.

3.2. One instance must be observed during 3-hour observation. Do not count instances of math discussed during formal teaching times (e.g., group time, math work time).

5.1. "Many" means 5 different materials for each age group. Credit should be given only for materials obviously designed for math learning.

5.2. No credit can be given for 5.2 unless 5.1 is scored "Yes."

5.3. In order to give credit for "well organized and in good condition," about 75% of the materials that are accessible should meet this standard.

5.4. One instance must be observed during free play, and one must be observed during a routine.

7.2. Score NA if only infant and toddlers are enrolled or if both preschoolers and school-agers attend only part day.

Questions

1.1, 3.1, 5.1, 7.1. In addition to what is out today, are there any other math materials that you use with the children? *If yes, ask:* Could you show them to me please? When are these used?

7.2. Do you ever do activities that help children learn math? *If yes, ask:* Can you give me some examples? How often do you do such activities?

Inadequate		Minimal		Good		Excellent
1	2	3	4	5	6	7

22. Nature/science*

1.1 No pictures, books, games, or toys accessible that represent nature realistically (Ex. animals only shown as cartoons or fanciful characters).*

1.2 No opportunities for children to experience the natural world (Ex. no exposure to trees, grass, or birds; no living plants or pets visible in home; no seashells or other natural objects).*

3.1 Some pictures, books, games, or toys that represent nature realistically appropriate for each age group to use (Ex. non-frightening posters showing real animals; realistic toy animals for younger children; nature/science magazines for school-agers).*

3.2 Materials accessible daily.

3.3 Some opportunities to experience the natural world daily, either indoors or outdoors.*

5.1 At least 9 different examples of appropriate nature/science materials with at least three of the four categories represented accessible daily for preschoolers and school-agers for much of the day.*
NA permitted.

5.2 Outdoor experiences with nature provided at least 2 times a week (Ex. infants placed on blanket on grass; toddlers explore flowers and trees in yard or park; children taken for walk where provider points out natural things; school-agers help in garden).*

5.3 Some daily experiences with living plants or animals indoors (Ex. plant in the room easy for children to see; provider points out trees, flowers, or birds from window; children observe aquarium).

5.4 Provider uses everyday events as a basis for helping children learn about nature/science (Ex. feeding and caring for pets and discussing why it's important; watching rain or snow with preschoolers and discussing the natural causes).*

7.1 Provider shows interest in and respect for nature (Ex. is caring with pets; helps children handle natural things carefully; helps school-agers with school science project).

7.2 Nature/science materials are well-organized and in good condition (Ex. collections stored in separate containers; animal cages clean).

7.3 Nature/science activities requiring more input from provider are offered for preschoolers and school-agers at least once every 2 weeks (Ex. cooking; simple experiments like measuring rainfall; sprouting and planting seeds).*
NA permitted.

(See Notes for Clarification and Questions on next page)

*Notes for Clarification

Item 22. Nature/science materials include 4 categories: *collections of natural objects* (e.g., rocks, insects, seed pods), *living things* to care for and observe (e.g., house plants, gardens, pets, butterfly garden, ant farm), *nature/science books, pictures, games, or toys* (e.g., nature matching cards, nature sequence cards), and *nature/science tools* (e.g., magnets, magnifying glasses, thermometers, prisms; for school-agers, test tubes with eye droppers, rain gauge, microscope).

1.1. If any nature/science materials are accessible to any age group, for one hour daily, score 1.1 "No."

1.2. If any children, in any age group, get to experience the natural world, score 1.2 "No."

3.1, 5.1. One example may be appropriate for more than one age group.

3.3. The intent of this indicator is that children are given opportunities to interact with nature. This can occur either by taking children outside to see or experience natural things such as trees, grass, and birds, or by providing experiences with nature indoors, such as through living plants, an aquarium, pets, and watching birds at a window feeder.

5.1, 7.3. NA permitted when only infants and toddlers enrolled.

5.2. To give credit for this indicator, the outdoor experiences children have must include living plants and/or animals.

5.4. To give credit, at least 1 instance must be observed during the observation.

Questions

1.1, 3.1, 5.1. Do children ever use any nature/science materials such as books, games, tools (like magnifying glasses), or collections of natural things? *If yes, ask:* Could you show me the materials, please? When do they use these materials? For how long are they out for use?

5.2. How often do children go outdoors? Could you describe any experiences they have with nature when they are outdoors?

Inadequate		Minimal		Good		Excellent
1	2	3	4	5	6	7

23. Sand and water play*

1.1 Sand or water play not available for children 18 months to 6 years of age.

3.1 Some sand or water play provided outdoors or indoors at least once every 2 weeks year-round.

3.2 Supervision of sand/water play is appropriate for ages and abilities of children.*

3.3 Some toys used for sand/water play.*

5.1 Sand or water play provided at least once a week.

5.2 Variety of toys used for sand/water play.*

5.3 Sand or water activities set up to facilitate play (Ex. not too crowded for toys; enough sand/water and space for number of children participating).

7.1 Sand or water play provided daily.

7.2 Different activities done with sand or water (Ex. on different days water used for washing dolls, floating toys, and pouring).

(See Notes for Clarification and Questions on next page)

Item 23. Mark this item NA if all children in care are younger than 18 months of age, and/or over 6 years of age.

Sand and water play require action on the part of the provider to supply appropriate materials for such activity. Allowing children to play in puddles or dig in dirt outdoors does not meet the requirements for this item. In addition to sand, other fine-grained materials that can easily be used for digging and pouring, such as bird seed, may be counted. Materials that pose a danger to children under 6 years of age, such as dried beans, small pebbles, styrofoam chips, corn meal, and flour, cannot be counted as a substitute for sand.

To give credit for sand/water, there should be a sufficient quantity of the material so children can dig, scoop, pour, and fill and empty containers.

Water play can be provided by using equipment such as a running hose, sprinkler, dishpans, or a water table. Swimming pools may also be used to provide water play. However, since pools pose serious health and safety risks, particular attention should be given to these issues in scoring Items 11. Health practices, 12. Safety practices, 27. Supervision of play and learning. Note that portable wading pools, hot tubs, saunas, and spas may not be used and cannot be counted as water play due to extreme health and safety risks. The health, safety, and supervision consequences of using sand or water with children of any age should be considered in Items 11, 12, and 27.

3.2. Infant/toddler sand and water play must always be closely supervised. If any eating or drinking of the play material is observed, score this indicator "No." If sand/water play is not observed, base score on supervision that is observed during other activities.

3.3, 5.2. Examples of toys for use with sand and water are kitchen utensils, shovel and bucket, small cars and trucks, floating toys, plastic containers.

3.3. "Some" means at least two toys.

5.2. For "variety," consider the *differences among the toys* that children can use. Variety is represented in toy characteristics, such as use, size, transparency level, shape, color, and these types of properties should be considered, but *use* of the toys is of prime importance in making a scoring decision. If only duplicates of one toy are accessible (e.g., many spoons), then the requirements for variety are not met. Variety in toys does not have to be provided all at one time—variety can be provided through regular rotation of toys. If the provider reports that toys are rotated, ask to see the other toys, and find out how often they are rotated. If both sand and water are accessible, variety in toys must be provided for both, but the same toys can be used to meet the requirement. *Number* of toys accessible for play is also considered when determining "variety." For example, when fewer children use the toys at one time, fewer toys are required for variety, as long as the toys can be used for different purposes. When more children must share, more toys of different types are needed.

Questions

1.1. Do the children ever use sand or water in their play? *If yes, ask:* Could you tell me how sand/water is used?

3.1, 5.1, 7.1. How often is sand or water play provided?

3.3, 5.2. Are any toys/equipment used for the sand and water play? Could you please describe or show them to me?

7.2. Are there any other activities or materials used with sand or water in addition to what I saw today? Could you tell me about them?

24. Promoting acceptance of diversity*

1.1 No evidence of racial or cultural diversity observed in materials (Ex. all toys and pictures are of one race, all print materials are about one culture, all print and audio materials are in one language).*

1.2 Materials showing diversity present only negative stereotypes.

1.3 Provider is observed to demonstrate prejudice against others (Ex. against child or other adult from different race or cultural group; against person with disability).*

3.1 At least 3 examples of racial/cultural diversity observed in materials (Ex. multiracial or multicultural dolls, books, pictures; music tapes or CDs from several cultures; in bilingual areas some materials accessible in children's primary language).*

3.2 Materials show diversity in a positive way.*

3.3 No prejudice is observed *or* provider intervenes appropriately to counteract prejudice shown by children or other adults (Ex. discusses similarities and differences; establishes rules for fair treatment of others).

5.1 Many books, pictures, and materials showing people of different races/cultures, ages, abilities, and gender in non-stereotyping roles (Ex. both historical and current images; males and females shown doing many different types of work including traditional and non-traditional roles).*

5.2 At least 4 examples of props representing various races/cultures accessible for use in dramatic play (Ex. dolls of different races; ethnic clothing; cooking and eating utensils from various cultural groups).*

7.1 Inclusion of diversity is part of daily routines and play activities (Ex. ethnic foods are a regular part of meals/snacks; music tapes and songs from different cultures included).

7.2 Activities included to promote understanding and acceptance of diversity (Ex. parents encouraged to share family customs with children; many cultures represented in holiday celebration).

(See Notes for Clarification and Questions on next page)

Item 24. When assessing diversity in materials, consider all areas and materials used by children, including pictures and photos displayed, books, puzzles, games, dolls, play people in the block area, puppets, music tapes, videos, and computer software.

1.1. To score "No," there must be at least 2 examples of materials that show racial or cultural diversity, that are obvious to the children, in the room used most of the time by them. 1 poster showing children of many races is counted as 1 example; 2 baby dolls of different races also count as 1 example, because they represent 1 contrast.

1.3. Score "Yes" only if there is obvious, deliberate, and repeated prejudice shown. Do not score "Yes" if one isolated example of "politically incorrect" or "culturally insensitive behavior" is observed (i.e., provider asks children to "sit Indian style"). However, in order to sensitize the provider, any such instance should be mentioned, for example in technical assistance associated with the scale.

3.1, 5.1. If materials are difficult to find or observe, do not give credit for 3.1 and 5.1. Count only materials that can be easily experienced by the children. Materials displayed do not have to be at the child's eye level to be easily experienced, as long as they are large and clear enough for children to see and understand.

3.2. If stereotyping or violence is shown with regard to any group, such as some toys that show "Cowboys and Indians" fighting, then this indicator should be scored *No.* Gender equity should also be considered here. When historical cultural traditions are represented, the images must be balanced with non-traditional modern representations. For example, if traditional African tribal cultures are represented in materials, then current representations must also be included. Look for problems that would be easily obvious to the children. It is not necessary to search avidly for negative examples.

5.1. For this indicator, at least 3 books, 3 pictures, and 3 other materials are required, and *all* categories of diversity listed need to be included to some degree. Materials must be located in spaces children use for much of the day. Materials located in spaces used only for relatively short periods (e.g., hallways, entry way, spaces used only early AM or late PM) are not counted to meet the requirements of this indicator. Do not count dolls because they are credited in 5.2.

5.2. To give credit, at least 4 examples must be accessible. At least 1 example must be appropriate for each age group. Examples include different kinds of dolls, puppets and block/dramatic play people, dress-up clothes, foods, eating and cooking utensils from different cultures.

Questions

7.2. Are any activities used to help children understand the variety of people in our country and in the world? Please give some examples.

Inadequate		Minimal		Good		Excellent
1	2	3	4	5	6	7

25. Use of TV, video, and/or computer*

1.1 Materials children are exposed to are not appropriate for ages of children (Ex. violent, sexually explicit content; frightening characters or stories; too difficult or too easy).*

1.2 No alternative activity is allowed while TV/video/computer is being used (Ex. all children must watch video at same time).

1.3 Children's exposure to TV, video, or computer is not limited (Ex. on all day; unrestricted access to internet).*

1.4 Television, video and/or computer used with children under 12 months of age. *NA permitted.*

3.1 All materials children are exposed to are appropriate for ages of children, non-violent, and culturally sensitive.*

3.2 At least 1 alternative activity accessible while TV/video/computer is used (Ex. children do not have to sit in front of TV and may go to other activity).

3.3 Time allowed for children 12 months and older to use TV/video or computer is limited appropriately for age of children.*

5.1 Materials children are exposed to are limited to those considered "good for children" (Ex. educational stories, music, dance, and exercise; computer games and videos that promote learning of many types).*

5.2 At least 3 interesting alternative activities accessible for free choice while TV/video/computer is used.

5.3 Provider is actively involved with the children in use of TV, video, or computer (Ex. watch and discuss video with children; monitor school-agers use of TV and internet; help children learn to use computer appropriately).

7.1 Most of the materials encourage active involvement (Ex. children can dance, sing, or exercise to video; computer software encourages creativity; school-agers make own video).

7.2 Materials used to support and extend children's current interests and experiences (Ex. video on snowman on snowy day; video showing children's everyday experiences; school-agers use computer to help with schoolwork).

(See Notes for Clarification and Questions on next page)

52

Item 25. Since infants and toddlers learn primarily through interactions and hands-on experiences with the real world, use of TV, video, and computer is not required. If TV, video, and computers are never used when children are present, score the item NA. If not observed, ask about the use of audiovisual materials.

Since new audiovisual media products are constantly being developed, consider all audiovisual materials or equipment used with the children, even if not named explicitly. For example, DVD materials and electronic games would be considered in scoring. Use of radio programs is also considered here, but not music.

1.1, 3.1, 5.1. Many of the audiovisual materials traditionally used with children and to which children are exposed in homes may not be appropriate for children. For example, many cartoons contain violence and anti-social behavior, and TV programs often have frightening content, encourage a desire for commercial products such as sweet cereals that are not good for children, and contain material that is beyond their understanding. To judge whether the content is appropriate and good for children, the observer should examine all audiovisual materials that the provider indicates are used with the children. In addition, when scoring these indicators include any exposure to audiovisual materials experienced by the children, even if not put on for them, such as news on the radio or on TV.

1.3, 3.3. Suggested time limits for media use vary with age of child. In a full-day program, TV/video is limited to 30 minutes a day for toddlers, 60 minutes a day for older children. Computer use is limited to 10 minutes for toddlers, 20 minutes for preschoolers, and 60 minutes for school-agers. Shorter amounts of time should be allowed if children are not present for the full day.

Questions

Are TV, videos, computers, or other audiovisual materials used with the children? *If yes, ask:* How are they used? How do you choose the materials?

1.2, 3.2, 5.2. Are other activities accessible to the children while the TV or videos are used?

1.3, 3.3. How often are TV, video, or computers used with the children? For what length of time are these available?

5.3. What do you usually do when children watch TV or use the computer?

7.1. Do any of the materials encourage active involvement by the children? Please give some examples.

7.2. Do you ever use TV, video, and computer materials to give information that relates to things that the children are interested in? Can you give an example?

26. Active physical play*

1.1 No outdoor or indoor space used daily for active physical play.*

1.2 Space (outdoor or indoor) used for active physical play is generally very dangerous (Ex. access requires long walk on busy street; unfenced area; insufficient cushioning under majority of climbing equipment).*

1.3 No appropriate equipment/materials for any age group in care.*

1.4 Equipment/materials generally in poor repair.

3.1 Some uncrowded space, outdoors or indoors, used for active physical play 1 hour a day.*

3.2 Spaces for active physical play are generally safe (Ex. sufficient cushioning under climbing equipment; fenced in outdoor area).*

3.3 Some appropriate materials/equipment suitable for each child in the group, including child with disabilities, if enrolled, used daily.*

3.4 Materials/equipment generally in good repair.

5.1 Outdoor area is used 1 hour daily year-round, weather permitting.*

5.2 Large outdoor active play area is not crowded or cluttered and is easily accessible.*

5.3 Ample materials/equipment for physical play to keep children active and interested.

5.4 All space and equipment (outdoor and/or indoor) are safe and appropriate for children who are allowed to use them.

7.1 Outdoor space has 2 or more types of surfaces permitting different types of play (Ex. one hard, one soft; grass, outdoor carpet, rubber cushioning surface, decking).*

7.2 Outdoor area has some protection from the elements (Ex. shade in summer; sun in winter; wind break; good drainage).*

7.3 Space for active physical play, outdoors and/or indoors, is organized so that different types of activities do not interfere with one another (Ex. play with wheel toys separated from climbing equipment and ball play; infants/toddlers protected from play of older children).

7.4 Materials/equipment used daily stimulate a variety of large muscle skills (Ex. crawling, walking, balancing, climbing, ball play).* *NA permitted.*

(See Notes for Clarification and Questions on next page)

Item 26. Active physical play requires that the children be active in order to develop their gross motor skills. Taking children for rides in strollers, swinging them in swings, or having them play in the sandbox should not be counted as active physical play. Non-mobile babies should be allowed to move freely to the extent that they are able, for example, on a blanket or other safe surface. Older children should be given developmentally appropriate opportunities to practice gross motor skills.

1.1, 1.2, 3.1, 3.2, 5.2. If several spaces are used, the area used most frequently should be given greater consideration in scoring.

1.3, 3.3. Appropriate equipment/materials must be safe for all children allowed to use them. For example, equipment/materials should not allow falls from high places, and have no sharp edges, splinters, protrusions, or entrapment hazards.

Examples of appropriate materials and equipment:
- **Infants**—outdoor pad or blanket, crib gym for younger infants, small push toys, balls, sturdy things to pull up on, ramps for crawling
- **Toddlers**—riding toys without pedals, large push-pull wheel toys, balls and bean bags, age-appropriate climbing equipment, slide, cushions or rugs for tumbling, tunnels, large cardboard boxes
- **Preschoolers**—climbing equipment, riding toys, wagons, balls, low basketball hoop
- **School-agers**—bicycles and other riding equipment, jump ropes, hula-hoops, equipment for ball games

3.1, 5.1. Less time is required for programs operating less than 8 hours a day. See "Explanation of Terms Used Throughout the Scale" on page 9 for time required for shorter programs.

5.1. For definitions of "daily" and "weather permitting" see "Explanations of Terms Used Throughout the Scale" on pages 10 and 11.

5.2. The outdoor space must be easily accessible to the adults and children who are currently a part of the program. Access should be considered for both typically developing children and those with disabilities, if enrolled. If there are 2 or more active play areas used with the children, score this indicator based on the average of what children experience.

7.1. Each type of surface (hard and soft) must be large enough to permit appropriate play.

7.2. Only one example of protection from the elements must be observed, but the protection must match the most prevalent adverse conditions caused by the elements in the local area.

7.4. Score NA if only non-mobile infants are enrolled. List 7–9 skills stimulated by the gross motor equipment.

Questions

Item 26. Are any areas used by this group for active physical play, including space indoors and outdoors? *If yes, and not observed, ask:* Could you please show me these areas? How often are they used, and for about how long?

Inadequate		Minimal		Good		Excellent
1	2	3	4	5	6	7

INTERACTION

27. Supervision of play and learning*

1.1 Supervision is usually not sufficient for age and ability of children (Ex. provider often leaves children and cannot see, hear, or reach them; children frequently unattended in dangerous situations).

1.2 Most supervision is punitive or overly controlling (Ex. yelling, belittling children, constant "No's").*

3.1 Supervision is usually appropriate for ages and abilities of children (Ex. infants/toddlers within sight and easy reach with only momentary lapses; provider stays outdoors with children).

3.2 Most supervision is non-punitive and control is exercised in a reasonable way.*

3.3 Provider actively supervises: other work or interests do not take away from care-giving responsibilities (Ex. housework done while children are asleep; telephone conversations kept brief).

5.1 Consistently careful supervision of all children adjusted appropriately for different ages and abilities (Ex. younger or more impulsive children supervised more closely).

5.2 Provider shows awareness of the whole group even when working with one child or a small group (Ex. provider frequently scans room when working with one child).

5.3 Provider reacts quickly to solve problems in a comforting and supportive way.

5.4 Provider participates in activities with children and shows interest in or appreciation of what they do (Ex. gives children help and encouragement when needed; helps child who is wandering to get involved in play; helps baby access toy on shelf).

7.1 Provider usually acts to avoid problems before they occur (Ex. brings out duplicate toys; moves active play before it disrupts quiet play).

7.2 Provider talks to children about ideas related to their activities (Ex. asks questions; adds information to extend children's understanding).

7.3 A balance is maintained between children's need to explore independently and provider's input into learning (Ex. child allowed to complete painting before being asked to talk about it; child allowed to discover that her block building is unbalanced before it falls).

---

*Notes for Clarification

Item 27. This item applies to both indoor and outdoor supervision. See "supervision" in "Explanation of Terms Used Throughout the Scale" on page 11. Since supervision of the various personal care routines is handled in the individual items, it is not considered here (see Items 8. Nap/rest, 9. Meals/snacks, and 10. Diapering/toileting).

To score this item, consider the number of children, their ages and abilities, and whether the provider is supervising the most hazardous areas/activities adequately.

1.2, 3.2. "Most supervision" means the majority (over 50%) of supervision that has been observed.

Inadequate		Minimal		Good		Excellent
1	2	3	4	5	6	7

28. Provider–child interaction*

1.1 Provider is not responsive to or not involved with children (Ex. ignores children; seems distant or cold).

1.2 Interactions are unpleasant (Ex. voices sound strained and irritable).*

1.3 Physical contact is not warm or responsive; harsh or inappropriate contact used (Ex. child jerked by arm; unwanted hugs or tickling).

3.1 Provider usually is responsive to children and is involved with them.*

3.2 Few, if any, unpleasant interactions; no harsh verbal or physical provider–child interactions.

3.3 Occasional smiling and talking to children throughout the day.

3.4 Some warm and responsive physical affection throughout the day in routines or play (Ex. holds child gently while reading a book; cuddles baby during bottle feeding; puts arm around school-agers while helping with homework).

5.1 Provider uses frequent positive verbal and physical interaction with children throughout the day (Ex. provider and children usually relaxed; voices pleasant; gentle touch).

5.2 Provider shows respect for children (Ex. listens attentively; makes eye contact; treats children fairly; does not discriminate).

5.3 Provider responds sympathetically to help children who are upset, hurt, or angry.*

7.1 Provider is usually sensitive about children's feelings and reactions (Ex. avoids abrupt interruptions; warns baby before picking him up; gives support to school-ager who had a stressful day at school).

7.2 Provider encourages the development of mutual respect between children and adults (Ex. provider waits until children finish asking questions before answering; gently stops baby from pulling provider's hair and says "this hurts").

*Notes for Clarification

Item 28. While the indicators for quality in this item generally hold true across a diversity of cultures and individuals, the ways in which they are expressed may differ. For example, direct eye contact in some cultures is a sign of respect; in others, a sign of disrespect. Similarly, some individuals are more likely to smile and be demonstrative than others. However, the requirements of the indicators must be met by the provider, although there can be some variation in the way this is done.

1.2. If only one or two brief instances are observed, and most interactions are neutral or positive, score "No."

3.1. "Usually responsive" means most of the time for each child who initiates an interaction or requires something. "Involved with them" means that the caregiver is not detached, seems interested in the children, and does not spend large amounts of time in tasks that are unrelated to child care and education.

5.3. "Responds sympathetically" means that the provider notices and validates a child's feelings, even if the child is showing emotions that are often considered unacceptable, such as anger or impatience. The feelings should be accepted, although inappropriate behaviors, such as hitting or throwing things, should not be allowed.

A sympathetic response should be provided in most, but not necessarily all, cases. If children are able to solve minor problems themselves, then a response from the provider is not needed. The observer needs to get an overall impression of the response of the provider. If minor problems persist and are ignored or if the provider responds in an unsympathetic manner, give no credit for this indicator.

Inadequate		Minimal		Good		Excellent
1	2	3	4	5	6	7

29. Discipline

1.1 Children are controlled with severe methods (Ex. spanking; shouting; confining children for long periods; withholding food).

1.2 Discipline is so lax that there is little order or control.

1.3 Expectations for behavior are usually inappropriate for age and developmental level of children (Ex. everyone must be quiet at meals; children must wait for long periods of time with nothing to do; provider becomes angry when infant cries).

3.1 No physical punishment or severe methods ever used.

3.2 Provider usually maintains enough control to prevent problems, such as children hurting one another, endangering themselves, or being destructive.

3.3 Expectations are realistic and based on age and ability of children with few, if any exceptions (Ex. sharing is not forced although it may be talked about; children not expected to wait for long periods).

5.1 Program is set up to avoid conflict and promote appropriate interaction (Ex. duplicate toys accessible; child with favorite toy protected from others; children not crowded; provider responds quickly to problems; smooth transitions).

5.2 Positive methods of discipline used effectively (Ex. attention given when children are engaged and behaving well; redirecting child from negative situation to other activity; timely intervention to avoid problems).

5.3 Attention frequently given when children are behaving well (Ex. provider watches, smiles, or participates while children are playing happily).

5.4 Provider reacts consistently to children's behavior.*

7.1 Provider helps children understand the effects of their actions on others (Ex. calls toddler's attention to other child's smiling face when offered a toy; explains anger resulting from knocking down other child's block structure).

7.2 Provider actively involves children in solving conflicts and problems (Ex. helps children use communication rather than aggression; provides words for non-talkers; helps older children talk out problems and think of solutions).*
NA permitted.

7.3 Provider seeks advice from other professionals concerning behavior problems.

*Notes for Clarification

5.4. There needs to be general consistency in the way the provider handles different situations and children. This does not mean that there can be no flexibility. Basic rules for positive social interaction in a group, such as no hitting or hurting, respect for others and for materials, should always be followed. A specialized program may be needed to help a child with a disability follow basic classroom rules.

7.2. Score NA if only infants are enrolled.

Questions

1.1. What methods of discipline do you use?

7.3. What do you do if you have a child whose behavior is extremely difficult to handle? Do you ever ask for help from others? *If yes, ask:* Can you give some examples of who might be asked?

Inadequate		Minimal		Good		Excellent
1	2	3	4	5	6	7

30. Interactions among children*

1.1 Interaction among children not encouraged (Ex. baby often kept isolated in swing or chair; talking among children discouraged; few opportunities for children to choose own playmates).*

1.2 Negative interactions among children either ignored or handled harshly.

1.3 Interactions among children often negative (Ex. teasing, bickering, fighting are common).

3.1 Interaction encouraged among children (Ex. non-mobile babies placed where they can interact with others; children allowed to move freely so natural groupings and interactions can occur).

3.2 Provider usually stops negative and hurtful interactions (Ex. stops name calling, fighting).

3.3 Most interactions among children are neutral or positive (Ex. calmly play next to each other; older children careful with babies).

5.1 Provider consistently models good social skills (Ex. is kind to others, listens, empathizes, cooperates; is polite to children and not "bossy").

5.2 Provider facilitates positive peer interactions among all children (Ex. places infants where they can watch and react to others; helps toddlers find duplicate toys; includes child with disability in play with others).

7.1 Provider points out and talks about instances of positive social interaction among children or between adults and children (Ex. praises child for comforting baby; recognizes child for getting duplicate toy instead of fighting; thanks older child for being helpful).*

7.2 Provider initiates some appropriate activities that give children experience in working or playing together (Ex. blows bubbles for several babies to watch together; teaches toddlers to roll ball to others; children help clean up together; older children encouraged to read to younger children).*
NA permitted.

---

*Notes for Clarification

Item 30. Score this item NA if no more than one child is enrolled to attend at any one time, or if two children are enrolled and one is absent.

1.1. "Interaction among children not encouraged" means that there is little support provided, either by the provider, schedule, or the environment itself, to help children play and communicate with one another. In some cases this is because the provider actively discourages interactions, for example, by:

- Requiring children to do their work or play alone, with no interruptions from others

- Requiring children to do the same thing at the same time, but with little communicating or playing together
- Maintaining very strict control, or a punitive atmosphere, that makes children too uncomfortable to interact with one another

Score 1.1 "Yes" when interaction among children is actively discouraged.

7.1. At least 1 instance must be observed.

7.2. At least 1 instance must be observed. NA is permitted if only infants are enrolled.

Inadequate		Minimal		Good		Excellent
1	2	3	4	5	6	7

PROGRAM STRUCTURE

31. Schedule*

1.1 Schedule is *either* too rigid, not satisfying needs of many children, *or* too flexible (chaotic), lacking a dependable sequence of daily events.*

1.2 Children's routine needs are not met (Ex. crying children; rushed mealtimes; delays in diapering; no snacks for school-agers).

1.3 Provider has no time to supervise children at play (Ex. all time taken up with routines or other interests).

3.1 Basic daily schedule exists that is familiar to children (Ex. routines and activities occur in relatively the same sequence most days).

3.2 Schedule meets the needs of most of the children.

3.3 At least one indoor and one outdoor play period (weather permitting) occurs daily.*

3.4 Both gross motor and less active play occur daily.

5.1 Schedule is individualized for infants, with some flexibility for toddlers and older children (Ex. each infant is on own schedule; toddlers eased into group schedule; outdoor play period lengthened in good weather).

5.2 A variety of play activities occur each day, some initiated by provider and some by children.

5.3 No long period of waiting during transitions between daily events.*

7.1 Schedule is individualized so that the needs of each child are met (Ex. tired preschooler allowed to nap early; school-ager gets own snack when hungry; schedule adjusted for child with special needs).

7.2 Most transitions between daily events are smooth (Ex. play materials for next activity set out before activity begins; children allowed to eat right after handwashing; provider keeps children actively involved to avoid troublesome behavior).

*Notes for Clarification

Item 31. "Schedule" means the sequence of daily events experienced by the children. Base score primarily on the actual sequence of events observed.

1.1, 5.3. Daily events refers to time for indoor and outdoor play activities as well as routines, including meals/snacks, nap/rest, diapering/toileting, and greeting/departing.

3.3. Both the indoor and outdoor play periods must each equal at least 1 hour in length for programs operating 8 hours or more. See "Explanation of Terms Used Throughout the Scale" on page 9 for programs operating less than 8 hours a day.

5.3. "Long period of waiting" means waiting without any activity for 3 minutes or more *between daily events* (e.g., running around aimlessly, whole group sitting at tables waiting for lunch, waiting in line to go out or to use the bathroom). Note that this indicator refers to waiting between transitions from one activity to another, rather than waiting within any activity.

Questions

5.1. Is flexibility possible in the schedule? *If yes, ask:* Can you give me some examples?

Inadequate		Minimal		Good		Excellent
1	2	3	4	5	6	7

32. Free play*

1.1 *Either* little opportunity for free play *or* much of the day spent in unsupervised free play.

1.2 Inadequate toys, materials, and equipment provided for children to use in free play (Ex. very few toys or toys generally in poor repair).

3.1 Free play occurs daily, indoors *and* outdoors, weather permitting.*

3.2 Some supervision provided to protect children's safety and to facilitate play.*

3.3 Adequate toys, materials, and equipment accessible for free play.*

5.1 Free play occurs daily for much of the day, some indoors and some outdoors, weather permitting.*

5.2 Provider actively involved in facilitating children's play throughout the day (Ex. helps children get materials they need; helps children use materials that are hard to manage).

5.3 Ample and varied toys, materials, and equipment provided for free play.*

7.1 Supervision used as an educational interaction (Ex. provider adds words to children's actions; points out interesting features of toys; encourages children to talk about activities; introduces concepts in relation to play).*

7.2 Provider adds materials to stimulate interest during free play (Ex. brings out toys not used earlier that day; rotates materials; introduces new activities to children).

*Notes for Clarification

Item 32. "Free play" means that a child is permitted to select materials and companions and, as far as possible, to manage play independently. Adult interaction is in response to the child's needs. Non-mobile children will have to be offered materials for their free choice and moved to different areas to facilitate access.

3.1. To give credit, children must be able to participate in free play for at least 1 hour daily in full-day programs of 8 hours or more. The 1 hour may take place at one time, or be a combination of times throughout the day. See "Explanation of Terms Used Throughout the Scale" on page 9 for time required for programs operating less than 8 hours a day.

3.1, 5.1. Free play or free choice does not require that all materials are accessible for children's choice. The number of activities may be limited as long as the children may choose where, with what, and with whom they play. For definition of "weather permitting" see "Explanations of Terms Used Throughout the Scale" on page 11.

3.2. Score "No" only when supervision is extremely lax.

3.3, 5.3. Materials must be made accessible to non-mobile children to be given credit.

5.3. "Ample and varied" means that children have many choices of appropriately challenging and interesting toys, materials, and equipment to use during free play so that each child can find a satisfying challenge.

7.1. At least 2 instances must be observed.

Questions

3.1, 5.1. What does the weather have to be like to allow the children to play outside?

7.2. Do you have any additional play materials for children to use? *If yes, ask:* May I see them please? How often do children get to use these?

Inadequate		Minimal		Good		Excellent
1	2	3	4	5	6	7

33. Group time*

1.1 Children usually kept together as a whole group (Ex. all do same art project, have story read to them, listen to records).*

1.2 Very few opportunities for provider to interact with individual children or small groups.

1.3 Activities done in whole groups are usually inappropriate for children (Ex. content too difficult; children not interested; activity lasts too long).

1.4 Provider often behaves negatively when children do not participate well in whole group (Ex. gets angry; sends child to time-out).

3.1 Some opportunity for children to play individually, or be part of self-selected small groups.

3.2 Activities done in whole group are usually appropriate.

3.3 Provider is positive and acceptant with children during whole-group time.

5.1 Whole-group gatherings limited to short periods, suited to age and individual needs of children.*

5.2 Many play activities done in self-selected small groups or individually.*

5.3 Alternative activities are accessible for children not participating in whole-group activity.

7.1 Whole-group activities are set up to maximize children's success (Ex. enough space so children are not crowded; active participation encouraged; book large enough so all can easily see).

7.2 Provider engages in educational interaction with small groups and individual children, as well as with the whole group (Ex. discusses what children are playing with; reads story).*

---

*Notes for Clarification

Item 33. This item refers to play and learning activities, not to routines. If children are never required to do the same activity as a whole group during play or learning, score this item NA. If no group activity is observed, but there is evidence that such activities are used with the children (Ex. circle time is listed on posted schedule; a group activity is shown on lesson plan), score the item based on information obtained by questions asked during the interview with the provider.

1.1. Whole group means all the children who are cared for together, doing the same activity.

5.1. One way to determine whether the whole-group gathering is suitable for the age and needs of the children is to observe whether the children remain generally interested and involved and no punitive methods are used to maintain the group.

5.2. To give credit for "many," at least half of the play activities observed should be completed in self-selected small groups or individually. Play activities do not include passive experiences such as sitting in circle, watching TV, or being required to complete specific assigned tasks such as worksheets.

7.2. At least 2 examples must be observed.

Inadequate		Minimal		Good		Excellent
1	2	3	4	5	6	7

34. Provisions for children with disabilities*

1.1 No attempt by provider to assess children's needs or find out about available assessments.

1.2 No attempt to meet children's special needs (Ex. needed modifications not made in provider interaction, physical environment, program activities, schedule).

1.3 No involvement of parents in helping provider understand children's needs or in setting goals for the children.

1.4 Very little involvement of children with disabilities with the rest of the group (Ex. children do not eat at same table; wander and do not participate in activities).

3.1 Provider has information from available assessments.

3.2 Minor modifications made to meet the needs of children with disabilities.*

3.3 Some involvement of parents and provider in setting goals (Ex. parents and provider attend Individual Family Service Plan or Individualized Education Plan meeting).

3.4 Some involvement of children with disabilities in ongoing activities with the other children.

5.1 Provider follows through with activities and interactions recommended by other professionals (Ex. medical doctors, therapists, educators) to help children meet identified goals.

5.2 Modifications made as needed in environment, program, and schedule so that children can participate in many activities with others.

5.3 Parents frequently involved in sharing information with provider, setting goals, and giving feedback about how program is working.

7.1 Most of the professional intervention is carried out within the regular activities of the home.

7.2 Children with disabilities are integrated into the group and participate in most activities.

7.3 Provider contributes to individual assessments and intervention plans.

---

*Notes for Clarification

Item 34. Note that this item is scored only if there is a child in the group with an identified and diagnosed disability, with a completed assessment. If the diagnosis and assessment have not been completed on the child (or if there is no child with a disability enrolled), score this item NA. If a child is receiving services, this can be accepted as evidence that a diagnosis and assessment exist. Existence of an IEP/IFSP is not required to score this item. To ensure privacy for families, the provider need not point out the child or tell the observer about the particulars of the disability. As you question the provider about how the identified child's special needs are handled, you do not need to know which child is being discussed.

3.2. Minor modifications may include limited changes in the environment (such as a ramp) to allow the children to attend, or a therapist who visits the program to work with the children periodically.

Questions

Could you describe how you try to meet the needs of the children with disabilities in your family child care home?

1.1, 3.1. Do you have any information from assessments on the children? *If yes, ask:* How is it used?

1.2, 3.2, 5.2. Do you need to do anything special to meet the needs of the children? *If yes, ask:* Please describe what you do.

1.3, 3.3, 5.3. Are you and the children's parents involved in helping to decide how to meet the children's needs? *If yes, ask:* Please describe.

5.1, 7.1. How are intervention services such as therapy handled?

7.3. Are you involved in the children's assessments or in the development of intervention plans? *If yes, ask:* What is your role?

Inadequate		Minimal		Good		Excellent
1	2	3	4	5	6	7

PARENTS AND PROVIDER

35. Provisions for parents

1.1 No information concerning program given to parents in writing.

1.2 Parents discouraged from observing or being involved in children's program.

3.1 Parents given administrative information about program in writing (Ex. fees, hours of service, health rules for attendance).*

3.2 Some sharing of child-related information between parents and provider (Ex. informal communication; parent conferences upon request; some parenting materials).

3.3 Some possibilities for parents or other family members to be involved in children's program.

3.4 Interactions between child's family members and provider are generally respectful and positive.

5.1 Parents urged to observe in family child care home prior to enrollment.

5.2 Parents made aware in writing of philosophy and approaches practiced (Ex. parent handbook; discipline policy; descriptions of activities; parent orientation meeting).*

5.3 Much sharing of child-related information between parents and provider (Ex. frequent informal communication; parent meetings; newsletters; parenting information available on health, safety, and child development).

5.4 Variety of alternatives used to encourage family involvement in children's program (Ex. bring birthday treat; eat lunch with child; attend family pot luck).

7.1 Parents asked for an evaluation of the program annually (Ex. parent questionnaires; group evaluation meeting).

7.2 Parents referred to other professionals when needed for the well-being of their child (Ex. for special parenting help; for health concerns about child).*

7.3 Provider and parents have a conference at least yearly to review child's progress and plan for the future.

---

*Notes for Clarification

3.1, 5.2. Materials must be easily understood by all parents. For example, translations provided in languages other than English, if necessary.

7.2. If provider reports no past need to refer to other professionals, give credit (score "yes") if she can tell you of appropriate resources in case the problem comes up.

Questions

1.1, 3.1, 5.2. Is any written information about the program given to parents? *If yes, ask:* What is included in this information?

1.2, 3.3, 5.4. Are there any ways that parents can be involved in their child's program? *If yes, ask:* Please give some examples.

3.2, 5.3. Do you and the parents share information about the children? *If yes, ask:* How is this done? About how often?

3.4. What is your relationship with the parents usually like?

5.1. Are parents able to visit before their child is enrolled? *If yes, ask:* How is this handled?

7.1. Do parents take part in evaluating the program? *If yes, ask:* How is this done? About how often?

7.2. Do you ever refer parents for help with the well-being of their child? *If yes, ask:* Can you give me some examples? *If no, ask:* Do you know of any resource in case this problem comes up?

Inadequate		Minimal		Good		Excellent
1	2	3	4	5	6	7

36. Balancing personal and caregiving responsibilities

1.1 Provider makes little or no changes in home, personal, or family responsibilities in order to care for children (Ex. housekeeping duties and errands outside the home interfere with caregiving responsibilities).

1.2 Child care responsibilities often interfere substantially with personal or family responsibilities (Ex. needs of own children and family for space and attention difficult to meet).

1.3 Children often left with unqualified substitute caregivers (Ex. older school-agers; adults who do not know the policies and practices required in the home; people unfamiliar to the children).

3.1 Some accommodations made by provider to meet basic caregiving needs for children.

3.2 Provider's primary focus during operating hours is on child care.

3.3 Child care responsibilities usually do not interfere with personal or family responsibilities.

3.4 Qualified substitutes are available and used as back-up help.

5.1 Family responsibilities and child care program seldom interfere with one another (Ex. space is specified for child care children and family members; special time for own child given after child care hours).

5.2 Consistent care is provided; substitutes rarely used.

5.3 Warm relationships between provider, provider's family, children in child care, and their parents enrich the children's child care experience (Ex. provider's school-age children read stories to preschoolers; provider's spouse plays ball game with children; grandmother helps with homework).*
NA permitted.

7.1 Provider uses household tasks as enjoyable learning experiences for child care group, when possible (Ex. lets children help make lunch; shop for groceries).

7.2 Coordinates good caregiving activities with family responsibilities (Ex. stops at playground on way back from an errand; pays personal bills while supervising nap).

Notes for Clarification

5.3. NA permitted if provider's family does not interact with child care group.

Questions

1.3, 3.4, 5.2. Do you ever use substitute providers in your family child care home? *If yes, ask:* How are substitutes selected? Do they receive any preparation to be able to take over for you? (e.g., visits prior to serving as substitute; knows health, safety, discipline, and other basic policies)

5.1. How do you manage your family, personal, and child care responsibilities?

7.1. Do you involve the children in your regular household tasks? *If yes, ask:* Can you give me some examples?

Inadequate		Minimal		Good		Excellent
1	2	3	4	5	6	7

37. Opportunities for professional growth

1.1 Provider does not take part in any professional development activities (Ex. no current books or magazines on child rearing available in home; attends no workshops or courses; not a member of an early childhood or child care association).

3.1 Provider participates in at least one formal professional growth activity each year (Ex. attends one professional workshop per year or participates in distance education).

3.2 Provider has some child- and family-related resources in the home (Ex. books on curriculum, magazines such as *Parent's Magazine, Young Children, Child Care Information Exchange*).

5.1 Provider regularly participates in at least two formal professional development activities (Ex. attends 2 workshops, takes on-line course, or has 2 on-site training visits each year).

5.2 Provider has at least 10 current professional resources in the home, including information on health and safety, child development, curriculum, and working with families.

7.1 Provider is an active member of an early childhood or child care professional group (Ex. attends meetings, workshops, and support groups).

7.2 Provider is working towards or has achieved a CDA, AA, or higher degree.

7.3 Provider has achieved official recognition for outstanding quality (Ex. NAFCC accreditation; highest level of state quality recognition).

Inadequate		Minimal		Good		Excellent
1	2	3	4	5	6	7

38. Provisions for professional needs

1.1 No access to phone in home.

1.2 No file or storage space for child care materials (Ex. business records, child emergency and health forms, curriculum materials).

1.3 No time set aside for maintaining business records and planning for child care.

3.1 Convenient access to phone.*

3.2 Access to some convenient file and storage space.

3.3 Two to three hours set aside monthly for maintaining business records, planning and preparing materials/activities for children.

5.1 Access to ample file and storage space.

5.2 Convenient space used for program administration and planning (Ex. portable file boxes used at kitchen table, desk with family computer that can be used when teenagers are not using it).

5.3 At least 2 hours set aside weekly for child care business and curriculum preparation.

7.1 Well-equipped office space for child care program (Ex. computer, answering machine used).

7.2 Convenient, well organized storage space so that extra child care materials and equipment are easily accessible.

7.3 Home has space that can be used for individual parent conferences that is conveniently located, comfortable, and private.

*Notes for Clarification

3.1. To give credit for this indicator, there must be a phone in the home that is easily accessible to all areas used for child care, including outdoors. A cell phone is acceptable if it is accessible, and can receive a signal where used.

Questions

1.1, 3.1. Do you have access to a telephone? *If yes, ask:* Can you show me?

1.2, 3.2, 5.1, 7.2. Do you have access to any file and storage space? *If yes, ask:* Can you show me?

1.3, 3.3, 5.3. Do you need to set aside any time to work on things related to your family child care home? *If yes, ask:* About how long does it take? About how often do you need to do this? *Follow up with more specific questions about record keeping and curriculum preparation.*

5.2, 7.1. Is there any space that you use for work on program administration and curriculum planning? *If yes, ask:* Could you please show me the space that you use? Is there any equipment that you use in addition to what you've shown me?

7.3. If you need to have a conference with a parent, when and where would you do this?

Sample of a Filled-in Score Sheet

20. Dramatic play

| 1 2 3 4 5 ⑥ 7 |

Y N		Y N		Y N NA		Y N NA
1.1 ☐ ☑		3.1 ☑ ☐		5.1 ☑ ☐		7.1 ☑ ☐
		3.2 ☑ ☐		5.2 ☑ ☐		7.2 ☐ ☑ ☐
				5.3 ☑ ☐		7.3 ☑ ☐
				5.4 ☑ ☐ ☐		

materials accessible all day

3.1, 5.1, 5.2. Dramatic play materials accessible (list for each age group):

Infants/toddlers: 5 dolls – some small, 2 toy telephones, 10 soft animals.

Toddlers and Preschoolers: dress-up clothes for men & women, child sized kitchen, cooking and eating props. and food, 2 small building with people.

7.1. Materials that represent diversity (list):
1) *dolls of 3 races, ethnic foods and clothing*
2) *doll house people include old couple and person with a walker*

7.3. Provider facilitates children's play (1 example observed)? (y)/n
suggests having a picnic and helps children find things continue to play picnic with group

21. Math/number

| 1 2 3 4 ⑤ 6 7 |

Y N		Y N		Y N		Y N NA
1.1 ☐ ☑		3.1 ☑ ☐		5.1 ☑ ☐		7.1 ☐ ☑
1.2 ☐ ☑		3.2 ☑ ☐		5.2 ☑ ☐		7.2 ☐ ☑ ☐
1.3 ☐ ☑				5.3 ☑ ☐		7.3 ☑ ☐
				5.4 ☑ ☐		

3.1, 5.1. Math and number materials accessible (list for each age group):

Infants/toddlers: rattles of different shapes, 3 hard page number and shape books, shape sorters, nested cups

Preschoolers: 2 number puzzles, shape puzzle, parquetry blocks, 2 number storybooks, 1 shape book

5.4. Provider talks about math/number concepts during: a) free play? (y)/n *asks to "count how many" several times*
b) routines? (y)/n *"five minutes" to clean-up*

22. Nature/science

| 1 2 ③ 4 5 6 7 |

Y N		Y N		Y N NA		Y N NA
1.1 ☐ ☑		3.1 ☑ ☐		5.1 ☐ ☑ ☐		7.1 ☐ ☐ ☐
1.2 ☐ ☑		3.2 ☑ ☐		5.2 ☑ ☐ ☐		7.2 ☐ ☐ ☐
		3.3 ☑ ☐		5.3 ☐ ☑ ☐		7.3 ☐ ☐ ☐
				5.4 ☐ ☑ ☐		

3.1, 5.1. Types of science/nature materials accessible (for preschool and school age):

- Collections of natural objects: _none_____

- Living things: _none_____

- Nature/science tools: _magnifying glass, 2 magnets___

- Nature/science books, pictures, games or toys: *2 books, realistic plastic farm animals and dinosaurs*

3.1. Types of materials accessible to infants and toddlers:
2 hard page realistic books (kittens, farm), farm animals

5.4. Provider uses everyday events as basis for helping children learn about science/nature?
(1 example observed): (y /(n))

SCORE SHEET–EXPANDED VERSION
Family Child Care Environment Rating Scale–Revised Edition
Thelma Harms, Debby Cryer, and Richard M. Clifford

Observer: _____

Observer Code: ___ ___ ___

Home: _____

Facility Code: ___ ___ ___

Provider(s): _____

Provider Code: ___ ___

Number of providers present: ___ ___

Number of children enrolled: ___ ___

Highest number of children family child care home allows at one time: ___ ___

Highest number of children present during observation: ___ ___

Time observation began: _3.0_ : _4.0_ □ AM ☑ PM

Time observation ended: ___ ___ : ___ ___ □ AM □ PM

Time interview began: _3.0_ : _4.0_ □ AM ☑ PM

Time interview ended: ___ ___ : ___ ___ □ AM □ PM

Date of Observation: ___ ___ / ___ ___ / ___ ___
                      m m   d d   y y

Number of children with identified disabilities: ___ ___

Check type(s) of disability: □ physical/sensory □ cognitive/language
                             □ social/emotional □ other:_____

Birthdates of children enrolled: youngest ___ ___ / ___ ___ / ___ ___
                                            m m   d d   y y

oldest ___ ___ / ___ ___ / ___ ___
        m m   d d   y y

Number enrolled in each age group:

Infants (birth through 11 mos.) _____

Toddlers (12 mos. through 29 mos.) _____

Preschool/K (30 mos. through 5 yrs.) _____

School-agers (6 yrs. through 12 yrs.) _____

SPACE AND FURNISHINGS

1. Indoor space used for child care

| 1 | 2 | 3 | 4 | 5 | 6 | 7 |

	Y	N		Y	N		Y	N	NA		Y	N
1.1	□	□	3.1	□	□	5.1	□	□		7.1	□	□
1.2	□	□	3.2	□	□	5.2	□	□		7.2	□	□
1.3	□	□	3.3	□	□	5.3	□	□	□	7.3	□	□
1.4	□	□	3.4	□	□							

7.3. <u>Accessibility</u>: a) Doorways ≥ 32" wide? (y / n)

b) Easy to use handles on doors (y / n)

c) Thresholds appropriate height/beveled if > ¼" (y / n)

2. Furniture for routine care, play, and learning

| 1 | 2 | 3 | 4 | 5 | 6 | 7 |

	Y	N		Y	N		Y	N		Y	N	NA
1.1	□	□	3.1	□	□	5.1	□	□	7.1	□	□	□
1.2	□	□	3.2	□	□	5.2	□	□	7.2	□	□	
1.3	□	□	3.3	□	□	5.3	□	□	7.3	□	□	
						5.4	□	□				
						5.5	□	□				

5.3. Examples of provisions that promote self-help used (at least 2 observed):
    1)
    2)

5.5, 7.3. Use of adult seating by provider observed (at least 1 example)? (y / n)

3. Provision for relaxation and comfort

1	2	3	4	5	6	7

	Y	N		Y	N		Y	N		Y	N
1.1	☐	☐	3.1	☐	☐	5.1	☐	☐	7.1	☐	☐
			3.2	☐	☐	5.2	☐	☐	7.2	☐	☐
						5.3	☐	☐	7.3	☐	☐

3.1. Soft furnishings used during observation? (y / n)

5.1. Soft furnishings accessible much of the day? (y / n)

5.3. Number of soft toys: _____

4. Arrangement of indoor space for child care

1	2	3	4	5	6	7

	Y	N		Y	N	NA		Y	N		Y	N
1.1	☐	☐	3.1	☐	☐		5.1	☐	☐	7.1	☐	☐
1.2	☐	☐	3.2	☐	☐		5.2	☐	☐	7.2	☐	☐
1.3	☐	☐	3.3	☐	☐		5.3	☐	☐	7.3	☐	☐
			3.4	☐	☐	☐						

1.2, 3.2. Is it difficult to supervise while children are in:

   a) sleeping areas?   (y / n)
   b) any play spaces? (y / n)

3.3. List hazards observed in space:
   1)
   2)
   3)

5. Display for children

1	2	3	4	5	6	7

	Y	N		Y	N	NA		Y	N		Y	N
1.1	☐	☐	3.1	☐	☐		5.1	☐	☐	7.1	☐	☐
1.2	☐	☐	3.2	☐	☐		5.2	☐	☐	7.2	☐	☐
			3.3	☐	☐	☐	5.3	☐	☐	7.3	☐	☐
							5.4	☐	☐			

5.3. Number of children 1 year and older enrolled: _____
   Number of pieces of children's work displayed: _____

5.4. Provider talks about display? (at least 1 example observed): (y / n) _____

6. Space for privacy

1	2	3	4	5	6	7

	Y	N		Y	N		Y	N		Y	N
1.1	☐	☐	3.1	☐	☐	5.1	☐	☐	7.1	☐	☐
1.2	☐	☐	3.2	☐	☐	5.2	☐	☐	7.2	☐	☐

5.1, 7.1. Space(s) set aside for privacy:

A. Subscale (Items 1–6) Score __ __   **B. Number of items scored __ __**   **SPACE AND FURNISHINGS Average Score (A ÷ B) __.__ __**

PERSONAL CARE ROUTINES

7. Greeting/departing

1 2 3 4 5 6 7

	Y	N		Y	N		Y	N	NA		Y	N
1.1	☐	☐	3.1	☐	☐	5.1	☐	☐		7.1	☐	☐
1.2	☐	☐	3.2	☐	☐	5.2	☐	☐		7.2	☐	☐
1.3	☐	☐	3.3	☐	☐	5.3	☐	☐				
			3.4	☐	☐	5.4	☐	☐	☐			

1.1, 3.1, 5.1, 5.3, 5.4, 7.2. Greetings observed (✓ = yes, ✗ = no)

	Child	Parent	Information shared
1	___	___	_____
2	___	___	_____
3	___	___	_____
4	___	___	_____
5	___	___	_____
6	___	___	_____
7	___	___	_____

8. Nap/rest

1 2 3 4 5 6 7 NA

	Y	N		Y	N		Y	N		Y	N
1.1	☐	☐	3.1	☐	☐	5.1	☐	☐	7.1	☐	☐
1.2	☐	☐	3.2	☐	☐	5.2	☐	☐	7.2	☐	☐
1.3	☐	☐	3.3	☐	☐	5.3	☐	☐			

1.2, 3.2. Cots/mats, cribs for children < 2 yrs ≥ 36" apart or solid barrier? (y / n)

5.2. *All* cots/mats, cribs ≥ 36" apart or solid barrier? (y / n)

Other issues (e.g., supervision, schedule):

9. Meals/snacks

1 2 3 4 5 6 7

	Y	N	NA		Y	N	NA		Y	N	NA		Y	N
1.1	☐	☐		3.1	☐	☐		5.1	☐	☐		7.1	☐	☐
1.2	☐	☐		3.2	☐	☐		5.2	☐	☐		7.2	☐	☐
1.3	☐	☐		3.3	☐	☐		5.3	☐	☐				
1.4	☐	☐		3.4	☐	☐		5.4	☐	☐	☐			
1.5	☐	☐	☐	3.5	☐	☐	☐							

1.3, 3.3, 5.3. Tables/highchair trays washed? (y / n) sanitized? (y / n) *[before meals]*
washed? (y / n) sanitized? (y / n) *[after meals]*

1.3, 3.3, 5.3. Handwashing
(✓ = yes, ✗ = no)

	Children		Adults
Before eating		Before food prep, feeding	
After eating		After feeding	

10. Diapering/toileting   `1 2 3 4 5 6 7`

	Y N		Y N		Y N		Y N
1.1	☐ ☐	3.1	☐ ☐	5.1	☐ ☐	7.1	☐ ☐
1.2	☐ ☐	3.2	☐ ☐	5.2	☐ ☐	7.2	☐ ☐
1.3	☐ ☐	3.3	☐ ☐	5.3	☐ ☐	7.3	☐ ☐
1.4	☐ ☐	3.4	☐ ☐				

Other related issues (e.g., supervision, interactions):

1.1, 1.2, 3.1, 3.2. Diapering procedure (every adult observed): (✓ = yes, ✗ = no)

Prep						
Proper disposal						
Wipe adult's hands						
Wipe child's hands						
Clean diaper area						
Sanitize diaper area						
Same sink sanitized						

Other issues:

1.1, 3.1. Same sink sanitized after toileting use? (y / n)

1.3, 3.3. Handwashing observed (✓ = yes, ✗ = no)

Adult								
Child								

11. Health practices   `1 2 3 4 5 6 7`

	Y N		Y N NA		Y N		Y N NA
1.1	☐ ☐	3.1	☐ ☐	5.1	☐ ☐	7.1	☐ ☐
1.2	☐ ☐	3.2	☐ ☐	5.2	☐ ☐	7.2	☐ ☐ ☐
1.3	☐ ☐	3.3	☐ ☐	5.3	☐ ☐	7.3	☐ ☐
		3.4	☐ ☐ ☐	5.4	☐ ☐		

3.2. Handwashing observed (✓ = yes, ✗ = no)

	Child	Adult
Upon arrival in home or re-entry from outside		
After messy, sand, or water play		
Before shared water play		
After dealing w/ bodily fluids		
After touching pets or contaminated objects		

12. Safety practices   `1 2 3 4 5 6 7`

	Y N		Y N		Y N		Y N
1.1	☐ ☐	3.1	☐ ☐	5.1	☐ ☐	7.1	☐ ☐
1.2	☐ ☐	3.2	☐ ☐	5.2	☐ ☐	7.2	☐ ☐
1.3	☐ ☐	3.3	☐ ☐	5.3	☐ ☐		

1.1, 1.2, 3.1. Safety hazards:

Indoor:

_____

Outdoor:

_____

A. Subscale (Items 7–12) Score __ __   B. Number of items scored __ __   **PERSONAL CARE ROUTINES Average Score (A ÷ B)** __.__ __

LISTENING AND TALKING

13. Helping children understand language

1	2	3	4	5	6	7

	Y N		Y N		Y N		Y N
1.1	☐ ☐	3.1	☐ ☐	5.1	☐ ☐	7.1	☐ ☐
1.2	☐ ☐	3.2	☐ ☐	5.2	☐ ☐	7.2	☐ ☐
1.3	☐ ☐	3.3	☐ ☐	5.3	☐ ☐	7.3	☐ ☐
1.4	☐ ☐	3.4	☐ ☐	5.4	☐ ☐		

3.1, 5.1. Talking during routines (examples):

3.1, 5.1. Talking during play (examples):

5.4. Examples of descriptive words used:

14. Helping children use language

1	2	3	4	5	6	7

	Y N		Y N		Y N NA		Y N NA
1.1	☐ ☐	3.1	☐ ☐	5.1	☐ ☐	7.1	☐ ☐ ☐
1.2	☐ ☐	3.2	☐ ☐	5.2	☐ ☐	7.2	☐ ☐
		3.3	☐ ☐	5.3	☐ ☐ ☐	7.3	☐ ☐
		3.4	☐ ☐	5.4	☐ ☐	7.4	☐ ☐ ☐

3.1, 5.4. Verbal responses from provider to children (examples):

3.1, 5.4. Non-verbal responses from provider to children (examples):

5.3. Children encouraged to communicate with one another (2 examples):

1)

2)

15. Using books

1	2	3	4	5	6	7

	Y N NA		Y N NA		Y N NA		Y N
1.1	☐ ☐	3.1	☐ ☐	5.1	☐ ☐	7.1	☐ ☐
1.2	☐ ☐	3.2	☐ ☐	5.2	☐ ☐	7.2	☐ ☐
1.3	☐ ☐ ☐	3.3	☐ ☐ ☐	5.3	☐ ☐ ☐	7.3	☐ ☐
		3.4	☐ ☐	5.4	☐ ☐	7.4	☐ ☐

1.1, 3.1, 5.1. Number of accessible books for each age group

1.2, 3.2. Number of books in disrepair: _____

5.1. Any inappropriate books (violent, frightening)? (y / n)
List:

5.2. Wide selection of books for each age group?

Races: _____

Ages: _____

Abilities: _____

Animals: _____

Familiar experiences: _____

Fiction: _____

Factual: _____

5.3. Provider reads to individuals/small groups? Observed at least 1 example: (y / n)

7.2. Provider uses books with children (2 examples):

1)

2)

7.3. Provider encourages children to read at their ability level (1 example):

1)

A. Subscale (Items 13–15) Score __ __   B. Number of items scored __ __   **LISTENING AND TALKING Average Score (A ÷ B) __.__ __**

ACTIVITIES

16. Fine motor

| 1 2 3 4 5 6 7 |

	Y	N		Y	N		Y	N		Y	N
1.1	☐	☐	3.1	☐	☐	5.1	☐	☐	7.1	☐	☐
1.2	☐	☐	3.2	☐	☐	5.2	☐	☐	7.2	☐	☐
			3.3	☐	☐	5.3	☐	☐			

5.3. Provider interacts with children during fine motor play (2 ex.):
1)
2)

3.1, 5.1. Types of fine motor materials accessible (for preschool and school-age):

- Building toys:_____
- Art/craft materials: _____
- Manipulatives _____
- Puzzles:_____

Materials for infants and toddlers? List: _____

17. Art

| 1 2 3 4 5 6 7 NA |

	Y	N		Y	N		Y	N	NA		Y	N
1.1	☐	☐	3.1	☐	☐	5.1	☐	☐		7.1	☐	☐
1.2	☐	☐	3.2	☐	☐	5.2	☐	☐	☐	7.2	☐	☐
			3.3	☐	☐	5.3	☐	☐		7.3	☐	☐ ☐
			3.4	☐	☐	5.4	☐	☐				

Score "NA" if all children in care are younger than 12 months of age

3.1, 5.1, 5.2.   Types of art materials accessible (for preschool and school-age):

- Drawing (required) _____
- Paints _____   1.2, 3.2. Any unsafe or toxic materials used? (y / n)
- 3-D _____
- Collage _____
- Tools _____
- Types of art materials for toddlers (list): _____

18. Music and movement

| 1 2 3 4 5 6 7 |

	Y	N		Y	N		Y	N	NA		Y	N
1.1	☐	☐	3.1	☐	☐	5.1	☐	☐		7.1	☐	☐
1.2	☐	☐	3.2	☐	☐	5.2	☐	☐		7.2	☐	☐
1.3	☐	☐	3.3	☐	☐	5.3	☐	☐	☐	7.3	☐	☐
						5.4	☐	☐				

3.1, 5.1, 5.2. Music materials accessible (list for each age group):

5.3. Informal singing observed? (y / n)

5.4. Times recorded music used:

19. Blocks

| 1 2 3 4 5 6 7 NA |

	Y	N		Y	N		Y	N		Y	N
1.1	☐	☐	3.1	☐	☐	5.1	☐	☐	7.1	☐	☐
			3.2	☐	☐	5.2	☐	☐	7.2	☐	☐
			3.3	☐	☐	5.3	☐	☐	7.3	☐	☐

Score "NA" if all children in care are younger than 12 months or older than 7 years of age

3.1, 5.1. Types of blocks accessible (list for each age): _____

3.1, 5.1. Types of accessories accessible (list): _____

7.3. Provider encourages/participates in block play (1 example observed)? (y / n)

20. Dramatic play

1 2 3 4 5 6 7

	Y	N			Y	N			Y	N	NA			Y	N	NA
1.1	☐	☐		3.1	☐	☐		5.1	☐	☐			7.1	☐	☐	
				3.2	☐	☐		5.2	☐	☐			7.2	☐	☐	☐
								5.3	☐	☐			7.3	☐	☐	
								5.4	☐	☐	☐					

3.1, 5.1, 5.2. Dramatic play materials accessible (list for each age group):

7.1. Materials that represent diversity (list):

1)

2)

7.3. Provider facilitates children's play (1 example observed)? (y / n)

21. Math/number

1 2 3 4 5 6 7

	Y	N			Y	N			Y	N			Y	N	NA
1.1	☐	☐		3.1	☐	☐		5.1	☐	☐		7.1	☐	☐	
1.2	☐	☐		3.2	☐	☐		5.2	☐	☐		7.2	☐	☐	☐
1.3	☐	☐						5.3	☐	☐		7.3	☐	☐	
								5.4	☐	☐					

3.1, 5.1. Math and number materials accessible (list for each age group):

5.4. Provider talks about math/number concepts during: a) free play? (y / n)

b) routines? (y /n)

22. Nature/science

1 2 3 4 5 6 7

	Y	N			Y	N			Y	N	NA			Y	N	NA
1.1	☐	☐		3.1	☐	☐		5.1	☐	☐	☐		7.1	☐	☐	
1.2	☐	☐		3.2	☐	☐		5.2	☐	☐			7.2	☐	☐	
				3.3	☐	☐		5.3	☐	☐			7.3	☐	☐	☐
								5.4	☐	☐						

3.1, 5.1. Types of science/nature materials accessible (for preschool and school-age):

• Collections of natural objects: _____

• Living things: _____

• Nature/science tools: _____

• Nature/science books, pictures, games, or toys: _____

3.1. Types of materials accessible to infants and toddlers:

5.4. Provider uses everyday events as basis for helping children learn about science/nature?
    (1 example observed): (y / n)

23. Sand and water play

1 2 3 4 5 6 7 NA

	Y	N			Y	N			Y	N			Y	N
1.1	☐	☐		3.1	☐	☐		5.1	☐	☐		7.1	☐	☐
				3.2	☐	☐		5.2	☐	☐		7.2	☐	☐
				3.3	☐	☐		5.3	☐	☐				

3.2. Supervision issues: 7.2. Different activities done with sand or water:
3.1, 5.1, 7.1. Sand/water provided? (✓ = yes, ✗ = no)

	Indoors	Outdoors	How often?
Sand			
Water			

3.3, 5.2. Toys/materials for sand/water play:

Score "NA" if all children in care are younger than 18 months of age and/or over 6 years of age

24. Promoting acceptance of diversity

`1 2 3 4 5 6 7`

	Y	N		Y	N		Y	N		Y	N
1.1	☐	☐	3.1	☐	☐	5.1	☐	☐	7.1	☐	☐
1.2	☐	☐	3.2	☐	☐	5.2	☐	☐	7.2	☐	☐
1.3	☐	☐	3.3	☐	☐						

3.1, 5.1. (Tally)

Diversity	Books	Pictures	Materials
Race/Culture			
Age			
Abilities			
Gender			

5.2. Dramatic play props that represent various cultures/races? List:

1)

2)

3)

4)

---

25. Use of TV, video, and/or computer

`1 2 3 4 5 6 7 NA`

	Y	N	NA		Y	N		Y	N		Y	N
1.1	☐	☐		3.1	☐	☐	5.1	☐	☐	7.1	☐	☐
1.2	☐	☐		3.2	☐	☐	5.2	☐	☐	7.2	☐	☐
1.3	☐	☐		3.3	☐	☐	5.3	☐	☐			
1.4	☐	☐	☐									

Score item "NA" if TV, video, and computers are never used when children are present.

1.1, 3.1. Any inappropriate materials used? (y / n) List:

3.3. Times children use TV/video:

Times used for computer:

3.2, 5.2. Alternative activities accessible (list):

---

26. Active physical play

`1 2 3 4 5 6 7`

	Y	N		Y	N		Y	N		Y	N	NA
1.1	☐	☐	3.1	☐	☐	5.1	☐	☐	7.1	☐	☐	
1.2	☐	☐	3.2	☐	☐	5.2	☐	☐	7.2	☐	☐	
1.3	☐	☐	3.3	☐	☐	5.3	☐	☐	7.3	☐	☐	
1.4	☐	☐	3.4	☐	☐	5.4	☐	☐	7.4	☐	☐	☐

1.3, 3.3, 5.3, 5.4. Any equipment/materials inappropriate/unsafe? (y / n)

1.1, 1.2, 3.2, 5.1. Appropriate indoor/outdoor space used? (y / n)

7.4. Skills stimulated by materials (list):

older infant/toddlers:

preschool–K:

school-age:

A. Subscale (Items 16–26) Score __ __   B. Number of items scored __ __   **ACTIVITIES Average Score (A ÷ B)** __.__ __

INTERACTION

27. Supervision of play and learning

`1 2 3 4 5 6 7`

	Y	N		Y	N		Y	N		Y	N
1.1	☐	☐	3.1	☐	☐	5.1	☐	☐	7.1	☐	☐
1.2	☐	☐	3.2	☐	☐	5.2	☐	☐	7.2	☐	☐
			3.3	☐	☐	5.3	☐	☐	7.3	☐	☐
						5.4	☐	☐			

28. Provider–child interaction

`1 2 3 4 5 6 7`

	Y	N		Y	N		Y	N		Y	N
1.1	☐	☐	3.1	☐	☐	5.1	☐	☐	7.1	☐	☐
1.2	☐	☐	3.2	☐	☐	5.2	☐	☐	7.2	☐	☐
1.3	☐	☐	3.3	☐	☐	5.3	☐	☐			
			3.4	☐	☐						

5.1. Examples of positive interaction: a) verbal:

b) physical:

29. Discipline

`1 2 3 4 5 6 7`

	Y	N		Y	N		Y	N		Y	N	NA
1.1	☐	☐	3.1	☐	☐	5.1	☐	☐	7.1	☐	☐	
1.2	☐	☐	3.2	☐	☐	5.2	☐	☐	7.2	☐	☐	☐
1.3	☐	☐	3.3	☐	☐	5.3	☐	☐	7.3	☐	☐	
						5.4	☐	☐				

30. Interactions among children

`1 2 3 4 5 6 7 NA`

	Y	N		Y	N		Y	N		Y	N	NA
1.1	☐	☐	3.1	☐	☐	5.1	☐	☐	7.1	☐	☐	
1.2	☐	☐	3.2	☐	☐	5.2	☐	☐	7.2	☐	☐	☐
1.3	☐	☐	3.3	☐	☐							

7.1. Provider points out positive interaction among children (1 example):

7.2. Provider-initiated activities that encourage children to work or play together (1 example):

See notes for clarification for when to score item "NA"

A. Subscale (Items 27–30) Score __ __   B. Number of items scored __ __   **INTERACTION Average Score (A ÷ B)** __.__ __

PROGRAM STRUCTURE

31. Schedule

| 1 2 3 4 5 6 7 |

	Y	N		Y	N		Y	N		Y	N
1.1	☐	☐	3.1	☐	☐	5.1	☐	☐	7.1	☐	☐
1.2	☐	☐	3.2	☐	☐	5.2	☐	☐	7.2	☐	☐
1.3	☐	☐	3.3	☐	☐	5.3	☐	☐			
			3.4	☐	☐						

5.3. Example(s) of children waiting 3 minutes or more:

32. Free play

| 1 2 3 4 5 6 7 |

	Y	N		Y	N		Y	N		Y	N
1.1	☐	☐	3.1	☐	☐	5.1	☐	☐	7.1	☐	☐
1.2	☐	☐	3.2	☐	☐	5.2	☐	☐	7.2	☐	☐
			3.3	☐	☐	5.3	☐	☐			

7.1. Supervision used as education interaction (2 examples):

1)

2)

33. Group time

| 1 2 3 4 5 6 7 NA |

	Y	N		Y	N		Y	N		Y	N
1.1	☐	☐	3.1	☐	☐	5.1	☐	☐	7.1	☐	☐
1.2	☐	☐	3.2	☐	☐	5.2	☐	☐	7.2	☐	☐
1.3	☐	☐	3.3	☐	☐	5.3	☐	☐			
1.4	☐	☐									

7.2. Educational interaction with small groups/individuals (2 examples):

Score item "NA" if children never do same activity as whole group

34. Provisions for children with disabilities

| 1 2 3 4 5 6 7 NA |

	Y	N		Y	N		Y	N		Y	N
1.1	☐	☐	3.1	☐	☐	5.1	☐	☐	7.1	☐	☐
1.2	☐	☐	3.2	☐	☐	5.2	☐	☐	7.2	☐	☐
1.3	☐	☐	3.3	☐	☐	5.3	☐	☐	7.3	☐	☐
1.4	☐	☐	3.4	☐	☐						

A. Subscale (Items 31–34) Score __ __   B. Number of items scored __ __   **PROGRAM STRUCTURE Average Score (A ÷ B)** __.__ __

PARENTS AND PROVIDER

35. Provisions for parents | 1 2 3 4 5 6 7 |

	Y N		Y N		Y N		Y N
1.1	☐ ☐	3.1	☐ ☐	5.1	☐ ☐	7.1	☐ ☐
1.2	☐ ☐	3.2	☐ ☐	5.2	☐ ☐	7.2	☐ ☐
		3.3	☐ ☐	5.3	☐ ☐	7.3	☐ ☐
		3.4	☐ ☐	5.4	☐ ☐		

36. Balancing personal and caregiving responsibilities | 1 2 3 4 5 6 7 |

	Y N		Y N		Y N NA		Y N
1.1	☐ ☐	3.1	☐ ☐	5.1	☐ ☐	7.1	☐ ☐
1.2	☐ ☐	3.2	☐ ☐	5.2	☐ ☐	7.2	☐ ☐
1.3	☐ ☐	3.3	☐ ☐	5.3	☐ ☐ ☐		
		3.4	☐ ☐				

37. Opportunities for professional growth | 1 2 3 4 5 6 7 |

	Y N		Y N		Y N		Y N
1.1	☐ ☐	3.1	☐ ☐	5.1	☐ ☐	7.1	☐ ☐
		3.2	☐ ☐	5.2	☐ ☐	7.2	☐ ☐
						7.3	☐ ☐

38. Provisions for professional needs | 1 2 3 4 5 6 7 |

	Y N		Y N		Y N		Y N
1.1	☐ ☐	3.1	☐ ☐	5.1	☐ ☐	7.1	☐ ☐
1.2	☐ ☐	3.2	☐ ☐	5.2	☐ ☐	7.2	☐ ☐
1.3	☐ ☐	3.3	☐ ☐	5.3	☐ ☐	7.3	☐ ☐

A. Subscale (Items 35–38) Score __ __   B. Number of items scored __ __   **PARENTS AND PROVIDER Average Score (A ÷ B)** __.__ __

Total and Average Score

	Score	# of Items Scored	Average Score
Space and Furnishings	_____	_____	_____
Personal Care Routines	_____	_____	_____
Listening and Talking	_____	_____	_____
Activities	_____	_____	_____
Interaction	_____	_____	_____
Program Structure	_____	_____	_____
Parents and Provider	_____	_____	_____
TOTAL	_____	_____	_____

Family Child Care Home: _____

Provider(s): _____

Observation 1: ___ / ___ / ___
             m / d / y

Observation 2: ___ / ___ / ___
             m / d / y

Observer: _____

Observer: _____

I. Space and Furnishings (1–6)

1. Indoor space used for child care
2. Furniture for routine care, play, and learning
3. Provision for relaxation and comfort
4. Arrangement of space for child care
5. Display for children
6. Space for privacy

Obs. 1 □   Obs. 2 □   average subscale score □

II. Personal Care Routines (7–12)

7. Greeting/departing
8. Nap/rest
9. Meals/snacks
10. Diapering/toileting
11. Health practices
12. Safety practices

□

III. Listening and Talking (13–15)

13. Helping children understand language
14. Helping children use language
15. Using books

□

IV. Activities (16–26)

16. Fine motor
17. Art
18. Music and movement
19. Blocks
20. Dramatic play
21. Math/number
22. Nature/science
23. Sand and water play
24. Promoting acceptance of diversity
25. Use of TV, video, and/or computer
26. Active physical play

□

V. Interaction (27–30)

27. Supervision of play and learning
28. Provider–child interaction
29. Discipline
30. Interactions among children

□

VI. Program Structure (31–34)

31. Schedule
32. Free play
33. Group time
34. Provisions for children with disabilities

□

VII. Parents and Provider (35–38)

35. Provisions for parents
36. Balancing personal and caregiving responsibilities
37. Opportunities for professional growth
38. Provisions for professional needs

□

Average Subscale Scores

SPACE AND FURNISHING
PERSONAL CARE ROUTINES
LISTENING AND TALKING
ACTIVITIES
INTERACTION
PROGRAM STRUCTURE
PARENTS AND PROVIDER

Scale columns: 1 2 3 4 5 6 7

NOTES

NOTES